Sustainable
In A
Circular World

SUSTAINABLE
— IN A —
CIRCULAR WORLD

DESIGN AND RESTORE NATURAL
ECOSYSTEMS THROUGH INNOVATION

PEGGY SMEDLEY

Specialty Publishing Media
First Published 2020
Copyright © 2020 Peggy Smedley

Print ISBN: 978-1-63760-569-1
Printed in the United States of America

About the Author

Peggy Smedley is an award-winning journalist and tech expert who is Founder and President of Specialty Publishing Media (SPM), while during her 25-year career she has extensively covered IoT, manufacturing, construction technology, and most recently she can be found leading the discussion on sustainability, circularity, and resiliency.

SPM publishes *Connected World* and *Constructech* as well as produces The Peggy Smedley Show. Peggy has collaborated on seven published books, in addition to authoring her own book, *Mending Manufacturing,* and she has proudly surpassed 700 podcasts on her weekly radio show. Each week she engages in lively discussions with guests from all over the world to talk about technology, trends, and whatever is impacting our world as it happens in the moment. She is passionate about helping inspire our next generation of skilled innovators as well as restoring our ecosystem through the use of advanced technology and more.

She was named one of the Top 100 Influencers by Onalytica and one of the 100 Women B2B Thought Leaders you Should Follow, and the recipient of the ASCE Excellence in Journalism Award.

Peggy resides in Chicago with her husband and two dogs. She has three adult children.

Learn more https://sustainablecircularworld.com

Dedications

To my husband Dave, the most amazing emotional rock, who has been there with me from the beginning, encouraging me every step of the way, all while we raised three awesome children, Christina, David, and Aaron. My family continues to be what drives me and what reminds me that we should never take for granted the blessings we are given from above. I love you all very much!

Table of Contents

Sustainable in a Circular World
Acknowledgments
Introduction: **1**
Sustainability intentionally maximizes the environmental, social, governance, and digital actions to fully engage its potential around a long-term motivational direction. These three components (environmental, social, and financial) come together to build up the digital age and lead to transformation, creating real change in society.

CHAPTER 1
Forces: **13**
There are several key forces shaping sustainability today including generational differences, the emergence of the "Screener" generation, social connections, and more.

CHAPTER 2
History: **46**
A historical look at the technological revolution including the Amazon Effect, Prime, showrooming, and ship it my way, among others, gives way to new innovations in sustainability.

CHAPTER 3
Circular: **61**
We are moving away from the throwaway economy to a more circular economy, as we are experiencing the American awakening and the move from linear to more innovative design.

CHAPTER 4

Sustainability: **112**

The book digs into the basics of sustainability including sustainability 101, governance, ESG three pillars, stewardship across generations, the supply chain, the Paris Agreement, generative families, giving back to the community, the Microsoft Way, and going global.

CHAPTER 5

Future: **168**

The world needs to move from a grey to a green economy fueled by design techniques that are sustainable in a circular economy. This movement needs to be invigorated by the next generation of innovators who are committed to circularity and sustainability.

References **197**

Acknowledgements **203**

Index **204**

Forward

We stand at a profound crossroads. The combination of climate change, loss of habitat, pollution, and other factors has led to what is broadly recognized as the sixth great mass extinction — a global event that is already underway and is accelerating. This represents an existential threat to our species and is the challenge of our generation.

As formidable as this challenge seems, we have many assets at our disposal to combat it. It's time to put them into action. First and foremost, any action we take must be founded in a clear understanding of the environmental changes that are occurring and their cause. The amount of knowledge amassed by environmental scientists over the last several decades is vast. While there is always more to understand, we have a firm grasp on the scope of the problem and what action is necessary to solve it. Next, this requires a worldwide acknowledgement of the problem and a unified commitment to urgent action — unless we all do more to address it the results will be catastrophic. Our awareness and activism increase with each new record warm year, unprecedented weather pattern, loss of species, and climate change related natural disaster — such as the wildfires that devastated many parts of the world in 2020. Last, we have a set of technologies available or in development that were not available to previous generations. Technology will be a great enabler as we imagine and engineer the solutions this challenge requires.

We are seeing public and private sector action start to take hold and build momentum. I'm fortunate to work for one of those companies in the private sector taking bold action: Microsoft has pledged to be carbon negative by 2030 (removing more carbon than we emit) and to remove all the carbon our company has ever produced by 2050. This will be done with a combination of nature-based solutions as well as technology-based solutions, for which we announced an investment of $1 billion dollars with our Climate Innovation Fund.

I have the great honor of being involved in some of the technology that will be pivotal in the fight against climate change and in creating a sustainable future. The Internet of Things (IoT) enables billions of devices to sense the physical world in realtime, providing unprecedented visibility into our environments. Edge computing enables software to run on these IoT devices and be managed centrally in cloud computing-based solutions, and artificial intelligence both in cloud solutions and on edge computing deployments enables us to use IoT devices to sense things that weren't possible before with sensors only. And finally, digital twins enables us to create digital replicas that are always up to date with entire physical environments. The combination of IoT, edge computing, AI, and digital twins is powerful. Together they unlock new levels of optimization, agility, and realtime control that can be used to reduce carbon output through increased efficiencies, to reduce pollution and environmental impact, and to reduce consumption of natural resources. They also allow us to track both past and present events, simulate possibilities, and help predict future events.

I've worked with Peggy for several years now and have always been impressed with her grasp of a broad range of technologies and their application. It is wonderful to see her applying her knowledge and passion to the challenge of our time with this new book. The pages ahead are filled with details on the forces at play along with case studies to illustrate them. I'm fond of the saying, "you can't solve a problem you don't understand." Thank you for seeking to understand.

Sam George
Corporate Vice President, Microsoft Azure IoT

INTRODUCTION

Sustainable in a Circular World
design and restore natural ecosystems through innovation

What Is Sustainability?
Sustainability is environmentally sound living without compromising the needs of future generations. Sustainability intentionally maximizes the environmental, social, governance, and digital actions to fully engage its potential around a long-term motivational direction. These three components (environmental, social, and financial) come together to build up the digital age and lead to transformation, creating real change in society. A culture that is supported by a true sustainable vision is untethered by market shifts and leads to continuity for employees and customers.

Achieving sustainability involves everyone. It requires everyone to think differently about our lives, the economy, and the world. It means making a transition in how we view the environment and want to improve our quality of life today and for the future. We have the innovation, technology, and the people to design a greener tomorrow.

A Sustainable Ecosystem

A sustainable ecosystem is the bedrock for any environmental, social, and financial discussions. This is where we see a new path for humankind to realize its full potential for change in eliminating bottlenecks and rejuvenating vision. This is where communities can transition or even establish a new direction led by biodiversity, information, data, resources, and action.

Humanity must unite to work hard for a common cause. These are the facts. That is why you hear so much about communities, generative families, and individuals focusing on production processes that are more efficient and use fewer natural resources—based on principles around the circular economy, resiliency, water scarcity, and even climate action.

Circular Economy

What is the circular economy? The Ellen MacArthur Foundation defines it based on the principles of designing out waste and pollution, keeping products and materials in use, and regenerating natural systems.

In the simplest of terms, we are using parts, pieces, and components that can continually be reused into the design of products or projects. This means less waste and it's truly regenerative.

All across the world, businesses, governments, and individuals are beginning to recognize the need to transition from the current 91% linear world of our take-make-waste approach to a healthier production and consumption process. Current waste—from plastics, textiles, food, and electronics—is having a negative impact on the environment and its natural resources.

As the glut of products continues to contaminate our world, plastics appears to be the most pronounced in a throwaway economy. Despite many efforts to curb plastic pollution, it continues to plague the ecosystem as one of the top environmental concerns. The conveniences in our disposable society has led to a single-use throwaway culture, which accounts for a disturbing 40% of all the plastic generated every year.

While there is still considerable concern, plastic recycling has seen a slight improvement. But the surfeit of plastics to landfills—this includes disposable packaging, biodegradable cellulose-based containers, shopping bags, and plastic bottles—seems to be never-ending. We are still dismayed by the stockpile of recyclable waste in our landfills, which are overrun with plastics and other junk.

Perhaps even more disconcerting is that plastic trash continues to find its way into our waterways and oceans. Environmentalists and individuals are sounding the alarm postulating that if we continue at the rate we are going, by 2050, plastic in the ocean will outweigh fish.

The world needs water. It's that simple. But our ability as humankind to supply clean freshwater isn't simple. While scientists might disagree about what is happening to the natural landscape, the inextricable truth is that billions of people around the world today still experience water scarcity during their lifetime. Water scarcity can be defined as the lack of fresh-water resources to meet the standard water demand, both quantity and quality.

Water scarcity can be caused by droughts, lack of rainfall, pollution, overpopulation, or when we simply abuse and consume way too much of it. While most of us living in North America cannot even imagine going without water on a daily basis, people in other parts of the world struggle with food shortages, as a result of water demand. They have no ability to irrigate their lands to generate their own food source for harvesting and drip irrigation.

Water scarcity greatly stresses arid regions around the world. As it rapidly intensifies, water scarcity will negatively impact agricultural production and drinking water availability as droughts escalate these regions.

While water cloaks 71% of our planet, and we might quickly assume it is in excess, freshwater—the water we drink to nourish our bodies, bathe in, irrigate our farm fields—is incredibly rare. Only 3% is considered fresh water, the remainder is too salty for growing crops, drinking, and is in frozen glaciers, or otherwise unavailable for our use. That means 97% of the earth's water is found in oceans. Water scarcity remains a consequential problem impacting millions, if not billions, of people globally.

Here's the point. Whatever your view, there is no getting around the water question that faces humankind. Ecosystems are becoming extremely strained. Rivers, lakes, and aquifers are drying up or becoming polluted. Many of the wetlands have disappeared. Climate change is altering patterns of weather and water around the world, causing shortages and droughts in some areas and floods in others.

Agriculture consumes more water than any other source. A quick calculation reveals much of the water is being wasted and the process has been inefficient for many communities. With a greater focus on advancement in technology improvements, water conservation is getting better, but not fast enough. We know these facts and individuals, coupled with technology, are working to address these challenges.

While resources are scarce, it is important to note that water scarcity is natural and permanent; while a water shortage is man-made based on market conditions and is temporary or can be altered.

Predicated on the current consumption rate, by 2025, two-thirds of the world's population may face water shortages. And ecosystems around the world will suffer even more.

Innovative methods must be applied for sustainable water use. Design, in-stream flows, and even freshwater species will be a geographic advantage, helping to create a more self-sufficient city or community.

Demands on increased water use have been growing on a global scale. By 2050, we can expect water demand will surge beyond the population and the economy, and water quality and resources will continue to present significant challenges. Part of the challenge is that water services are not keeping pace with the ability to be as sustainable as the demands of the environment.

As a society, we face many challenges to reduce poverty and protect the forests, natural resources and species, water, energy, climate, and the ocean.

Again, like anything else, simple math says if we are going to find our human potential in solving these global problems, we need to first acknowledge what is required of governments, businesses, and individuals in order to adequately address these objectives.

It's more than saying we will do something. It's about actually monitoring and measuring short and long-term economic results. The sustainability problems are heavily weighted, maximizing our potential on doing something that our innovators find rewarding.

Our Pillars to Success

Many are questioning why government and industry continue to make the same missteps as past civilizations. National and tribal governments need to make the necessary investments in their local communities to address the many aberrations that are endangering humanity and tackle the hazards, amplified by environmental changes.

That means we need to consider where and how we build our communities. What is the ecological damage or harm to the communities by these decisions (flooding, wildfires, etc.)? If a society cannot learn from history, it is doomed to repeat the same miscalculations.

This means addressing resiliency in design, creating economic incentive or proactive management, reviewing current funding mechanisms, analyzing existing regulatory decisions, and encouraging innovation in development.

Companies will need to create a framework for financial decisions that display true data or taxonomy of clarity. Simply, you can't change what you can't measure. This information will need to depict how business models will allow for sustainability in a circular economy and for deep financial growth. Investors want true transparency to determine new movers, like the Tesla's of the world, are showing dramatic growth in clean energy and electric vehicles for the future.

Think about capital expenditures (CapEx) and all the monies being applied to acquire, upgrade, and maintaining plants, buildings, or equipment. Organizations need to better respond to innovations in energy management (i.e., autonomous grids and renewable energy sources) as part of everyday operational expenditures (OpEx) and day-to-day activities. This requires creating the necessary data models for today's investors who are specifically examining performance based on environment, social, and governance (ESG), but let's not forget digitization that is leading to strong operational results and high returns.

The future of business rests solely on the strength of sustainability efforts. Companies need to demonstrate a more efficient way in managing risk to be more cost-effective as they digitize their businesses. It will not be a separation of business, but part and parcel of everyday business. Thus, the most successful company needs to manage risk and understand how the company is going about improving on those risks. For instance, how is the company working to increase its contributions in social injustice and inequality?

The criteria are used in helping educate the company, training employees, and evaluating any risks it and all its employees might face in managing those risks in the future.

Lessoned Learned

Our world is quickly becoming endangered. We are depleting our natural resources all in an effort to enjoy our modern-day comforts. As companies, governments, and individuals, we must take a step back and figure out how to continue to enjoy our conveniences without exhausting natural resources.

The rapid rise in inequality, poverty, extremism, populism, coupled with water shortages, deforestation and other ecological degradation, and climate change, are drastically leading to the destruction of the planet's natural resources. All of these indications point to society and its production processes being eroded and reaching capacity.

While there is much discord on how to address these challenges. Industry and government are beginning to see that more exploitation is not the answer. It is time to restore integrity to the earth's natural system (zero-carbon energy, transportation, food/waste, and fulfillment). Now is the time to stem the tide of destruction for what is proving to be more than just unsustainable actions.

Many of you are just beginning to realize the impact you and your organization or community can make. As we continue to see the birth of new innovation, it will hold the promise of solving more problems.

Each generation has a view of what can be done. There are always outliers, those people who think outside the traditional bell curve of that generational norm. For the purpose of creating real environmental change, it will be anyone and everyone who sees themselves as wanting to make a difference. For the purposes of this encounter, we will focus on socially engaged individuals, and their generational outliers.

As new technology proves to be more disruptive and in the foundation of everyday life it will become even more meaningful and inspiring for greater tech advancement. As a result, that will lead to new business benefits in the form of reduced costs and adding more disposable income and building stronger customer ties.

Companies need to recognize that advances in technology will lead to a rapid collapse in our society if sustainable actions are not set-in place. This means adding transparency and other tools to manage and monitor sustainability processes for a positive impact on humankind.

We need to acknowledge the world is experiencing deep fundamental changes all driven by ecological advancements that are creating consequential environmental changes in our humanity driven by digital solutions. This destabilization is disrupting ecological sustainability patterns and processes.

Sustainability principles must be at the forefront of authorities and communities to renew and design cities and human dwellings that foster community cohesion and personal security to stimulate innovation, employment, and financial growth. My goal is to examine the impacts of urban activities, financial, social, and environmentally sound management and the safe reduction and recycling of waste and more efficient use of water and energy.

Sustainable Future

Sustainability is really about leaving something for the next generation. Drilling down even further, at the most basic level, it's all about being more sustainable through development practices, as it relates to being outstanding eco-friendly citizens in a global society. From a big picture, 30,000-foot perspective, think preservation, saving the forest, cleaner air, economic equity. At the end of the day, it's enriching society and, most importantly, reducing, respecting, and nurturing the natural environment.

A sustainability mission isn't altered when times are good or bad. A pandemic (like COVID-19) shouldn't alter employees from fulfilling any tasks previously set forth or following a corporate mission. The sustainability mission is supported by good data and is fixed into everyone's efforts. The data will provide the perspicacity to unleash the human spirit to continue to look at every aspect of growth that impacts life and society.

This means examining capitalism and the challenges in government and industry—and how those decisions positively impact and align with the cultural cause of the organization and society. Data will and should play a pivotal role, but energy, culture, and human desire cannot be overlooked.

Transformations in financial, social, and environmental—all driven by digital during the next decade—will create unprecedented challenges, all while creating new, amazing opportunities. The next decade will prove to be a "Turning" in bringing critical changes to the world for ushering like-mindedness and forging new pathways to addressing environmental needs through a common sustainable and circular economy.

We cannot ignore the possibilities that exist in the human spirit. We have the good fortune to realize a new trajectory involving human and system intelligence to elevate humanity. Therefore, the desire to be more globally competitive must be encouraged. Sustainability must be for everyone, not just the environmentalists. We have the ability to organize for a common purpose to apply innovative technologies to end poverty, inequality, and environmental destruction, and strive for a greener and circular prosperity for all.

CHAPTER 1

FORCES

Our World

Societies have experienced extraordinary growth. This footprint covers billions of people that have created significant societal, environmental, financial, and digital concerns across the entire world. Early signs of breakdown have resulted in organizations across the globe recognizing that disruptive technologies could have a profound impact on information, food, energy, transportation, and materials, altering civilizations for years to come. There is a confluence of forces directing humankind to consider ecosystems, sustainability, carbon reduction, climate change, soil degradation, economic inclusion, water scarcity, deforestation, local hiring, diversity, and the circular economy.

Much like the Industrial Revolutions that have come before them, the world is rapidly experiencing an urban revolution. More and more people are flocking to urban living environments. Setting-aside the COVID-19 pandemic for a moment since the long-term trajectory of urban living is still largely unknown.

Looking back in time, civilizations that have adapted, leaned-in organizationally, as well as technologically, have been the ones that have stood the test of time. It took grit. Many doubted whether an enormous cultural shift would occur. There has never been so much riding on the success of environmental and societal change like there is today.

Change has to be a process that spans everything humankind does across the world. People will have to embrace this metamorphosis and recognize the more they do to improve humankind, the better the world will become. It must be the belief that real strength comes from diversity as a society. People must feel protected, trust their neighbors, civic inclusiveness, help the most vulnerable, and build a better tomorrow, all while protecting the environment for future generations.

Each generation ages into the next generation. The length of time for this development is roughly what is required to become an adult. During this period, we all have shared experiences, which influence and shape our behaviors and sway our membership into a generation. Ultimately, these life moments in time all become burned into our consciousness. For instance, I can vividly recall one of the darkest days in the United States history as if it were a silent motion picture movie playing over and over again in my head. I was attending a trade show in Houston when the terror attacks on Sept. 11, 2011 occurred and I am certain many other people have the same flashback recalling where they were that day. Recognizing social cohesion thrives on community, capital, mobility, and the ecosphere. It's all about the connectedness.

Generations are shaped by life occurrences. Think of it this way. Nordstrom, for instance, does not promote its service to the outside world. Yet, its reputation for service is known to people as far away as Caracas and Mumbai. According to author Robert Spector of the book *The Nordstrom Way to Customer Service Excellence, 2012,* he says rather than being "customer-focused, it's more customer-driven."

In our workforce today, we have as many as five generations to consider for the first time in history (although there are varying schools of thought on the matter, of which we will address later in this book)—all with differing views about the world. But interestingly, and perhaps more importantly, they have some overarching values that cross generations. To further illustrate what works for each generation and cross generationally, we can better identify and overcome conflicts, shifting values, and environmental priorities of the various generations, and work toward collaboration for decades to come.

September 11The gravity of the climate problem has risen to the highest levels in corporations and government and financial institutions. Now we are seeing a greater push away from grey and dirty to green and lush. Could this be a new decade of restoration?

Solving the world's environmental problems will not happen overnight. The emotional impact is powerful, and it is having an enormous societal impact. And we are seeing more and more corporations changing their brands and influencing their leadership. These leaders recognize their role in a global economy and are now placing greater emphasis on environmental issues, circular economy, resiliency, and corporate sustainability. And with each generation the climate discussion gets a little louder.

Five Generations

A generation is a series of consecutive births. For the purposes of this book, we are going to examine five consecutive generations that have observable patterns that will prove deeply rewarding for future generations. The five generations we will be reviewing are the Silent Generation otherwise referred as Traditionalists. We will then look at Baby Boomers, Generation X, and Generation Y, or as they are more celebrated as Millennials, and Generation Z, cited by many names, which we will examine further.

Traditionalists—as they are known—are the generation that have mostly retired, with perhaps a few exceptions, and they are not convinced any of these global changes will happen in their lifetime. We will also take a closer look at the Baby Boomers that are expected to retire before the end of the decade. In addition, this book will also take a deep look at the younger generations. These generations encompass, Gen X, Y, and Z generations. These are the socially engaged generations that are driving much of the environmental movement. They are all highly passionate about making the world a better place. Admittedly, they openly share on Twitter, Snapchat, Instagram, and TikTok, and the information they are consuming is growing everyday across the globe.

Taking a Step Back

Because Millennials love to be engaged socially, it's no wonder that Traditionalists all over the world repeat the sentiment this generation doesn't get "it." Perhaps if we set aside our own biases, we can understand the stereotypes of each generation.

In all of mankind, this is perhaps the first generation to demand instantaneous information to be available at their fingertips through their mobile devices as part of their everyday life. While Millennials need information, their younger counterparts can't live without instant access 24/7. And that's why today's technology is not shaping a generation, but rather young consumers are shaping technology.

In their book *The Fourth Turning,* Neil Howe and William Strauss made the point that during the last five centuries history can be explained with a generation that lasts about 20-25 years and ends in a Turning. Simply, discussing generations is not new. There are four generational archetypes. These archetypes run sequentially in a fixed pattern every 80-100 years, mirroring the length of a human life, otherwise known in Canon Law of the Roman Catholic Church as the "Saeculum."

Each generation is determined by those born within a 20-year period and have resulted in what Howe calls "Great Awakenings," which have revitalized culture, art, and society immediately following a crisis. We might say that China is experiencing a Fourth Turning as a world power in manufacturing and military, coupled with the overall paradigm shift that is occurring in that country.

The four historical Turnings are: High (First Turning), Awakening (Second Turning), Unraveling (Third Turning), and Crisis (Fourth Turning). Think of it this way, historical events create the symmetry of a generation from childhood, young adults, parents and midlife leaders, to old age (these are the generations that shape history).

For instance, each generation reaches an apex of influence when it enters midlife and assumes a leadership role within society. One of the key takeaways is understanding each generation. For instance, Howe goes to great lengths to explain each generation and how it interprets the same experiences from generation to generation. Perhaps even more interestingly is his understanding of the differences in how each generation views an experience of the same event. He views these differences as extraordinarily unique. As a result, you begin to notice certain patterns and realize generations always follow other generations.

If the same generations are following other generations, then they must be following history itself. So, what we are witnessing is generations shaping history. History itself must be following this same pattern. This is how Howe explains it. If you go another human lifetime, you will get the American Revolution. You go along in a lifetime, you follow trends, such as, the Civil War. And then again, the same interval you get the New Deal in World War II. At this point, this was a decisive moment historically both constitutionally and economically. We all saw the birth of a world power in the 1930s and early 1940s.

If you believe in what Howe is espousing after these crucial moments, we all are part of these transformations in what he calls the outer world of civic life, politics, and economics, creating the Great Awakenings in American history.

After two decades, a new generation moves up to assume the midlife responsibilities, and the earlier generation takes on a less influential elderhood role. In society at this point, there is a culture shift. As each generation experiences the cycle of birth, growth, maturity, and then eventually death, the lifecycle of humankind repeats itself. The real question then is do you believe the 1960s and the 1970s were Americas fourth and fifth Great Awakenings?

Building on Howe's catalyst of the Fourth Turning, in my estimation the next 10 years will be pivotal for how we address the ecosystem. Environmental issues will take center stage for the next great leaders recognizing the importance to the shift in influential elderhood that is occurring—while not ignoring the pandemic of 2020, economic crisis, and the U.S. relationship with China.

Going back to the earlier discussion on Turnings then, it's interesting to note how they continue to catch generations by surprise. People talk about change, but when it happens, it disrupts the flow of life and generally people do not handle the transition well. In fact, while we all aspire to change, it creates considerable disruption and disorder. The real question that has yet to be answered based on Howe's assumptions is whether we are in a crisis or whether we are actually in a Turning?

Generational Differences

Looking at history once more, there is no question since the Industrial Revolution the world has changed significantly and the division between generational eras has only increased exponentially with the birth of the information age, the internet, and digital communication. But is the pendulum swinging back? With so many individuals and diverse generations still in the workforce, are we in a workforce and an environmental crisis?

The digital divide has created greater differences and has also shaped some interesting generational identities. Thus, the way people view the world in some ways depends on your age. Today, there are actually five generations that have an active decision-making role in the consumer marketplace and in the workforce, which has never before happened in our history.

	Common Name	Birth Years	Average Age
	Greatest Generation	1901 - 1924	
	Traditionalists/ Silent Generation	1925 - 1942	78-95 years old
	Baby Boomers	1943 - 1960	60-77 years old
	Generation X	1961 - 1981	39-59 years old
	Millennials (Y)	1982 - 2004	16-38 years old
	Screeners/ Generation Z	2005 - 2019	0-15 years old

The Greatest Generation is believed to provide Americans with much of the freedoms it enjoys today. Although this generation is not in the workforce now, we really can't talk about the other five without highlighting what this generation sacrificed for all the rest. Through its persistence and extraordinary character after World War II, the Greatest Generation is credited as saving the U.S. from Authoritarianism, Communism, and Nazism.

Enlisted men bravely served the army during World War II. To this day, my father still regales stories of his Uncle Chuck, his mother's younger brother, who went on to fight in World War II. Having served in the U.S. Armed Forces, he was awarded the Silver Star Medal—the third-highest decoration for valor in combat—after being held as a prisoner of war. He also received the Purple Heart for heroism after being wounded during the war and persevering even more, earning him the Bronze Star Medal for exceptional courage in combat. These are the sacrifices this generation made during a very crucial moment in history.

They grew up in the Great Depression. Hearing only stories of how this period devastated a generation, many young men were called up to serve in World War II. But they were not alone. Both men and women—while not in active military service—were employed in some capacity to aid the war effort. While the men served on the front lines, women were at home helping as farmers, miners, doctors; building planes, submarines, and infrastructure; or caring for the wounded. This was a war where everyone recognized their patriotic duty. They recognized their responsibility and realized they had to do something.

Even news commentator and journalist Thomas Brokaw asserted this generation was united not only by a common purpose, but also by common values, which is what led them to build a modern America. Regardless of being born and raised during a war and economic depression, this generation still found a way to persevere. As my 95-year-old mother-in-law recalls, these were historic challenges and achievements of a magnitude the world had never before witnessed.

She says, it was really the dedication of the men and women during times of war and peace that ultimately shaped the United States. My father-in-law William was flying a B-17 Bomber as a pilot in the U.S. Army Air Corps., when she was at home with the first two of seven children building what she calls today a "good" life. This generation worked for the family and enjoyed spending as much time as possible appreciating the little things. This was a generation that made popular the likes of musicians such as Miles Davis, Ella Fitzgerald, Duke Ellington, and Louis Armstrong.

Money is important. This is a generation that not only survived but thrived making dramatic advances in science and creating social programs that are still in place today. Simply, it was the Greatest Generation that built the United States into a global superpower and gave birth to the Traditionalists, or as it has also been defined the Silent Generation.

When we talk to older adults, we appreciate traditions and the stories that families write together. This is a generation that likes to add value to society. In my mother-in-law's twilight years, she does not like to dwell on the hardships of living in small places or having little money while her husband served in the military. Rather, she was determined to tell us all wonderful stories with a great sense of pride. In one vignette, she describes pound parties—and not the version in urban dictionary—where everyone shared a pound of some sort of food with another family.

The Traditionalists are the children that grew up too young to participate in World War II, witnessed the first satellite known as Sputnik, and the resulting launch of the space age. They were a group of individuals that were too old to partake in hippie fashions that resulted from a social phenomenon resulting from the 1967 Summer of Love (not to be mistaken for the riots in 2020). Ray Charles, Buddy Holly, Jackie Wilson, Fats Domino, and Little Richard sang their way into people's hearts.

Baby Boomers

It wasn't until just recently that the Baby Boomer generation had to relinquish its dominance as the largest generation in American history. Many still accede this group as perhaps the most influential generation in history (although there is some discord as to this assertion). While this generation is known for the civil rights movement, the second wave of the feminist movement, Woodstock, and the Vietnam War, as it moved into midlife, it became more fluent in how to use cellphones and laptops. This is a generation that works hard and saw age equaling seniority.

They are also the most successful, having created tremendous wealth, opportunity, and felt a great sense of solidarity. Author Howe compared this period in time to a season. He said the first journey is the spring era, which is really an American high, which actually corelates to how everyone was feeling in a post-crisis era with U.S. President Dwight D. Eisenhower (a distant cousin of my husband's family) and John Kennedy at the helm. It was barbecues and apple pie time in American history.

By the 1960s, we started to see a shift. There were protests and rebellions and many student unions were formed. This was the birth of individualism. This is a generation that listened to Elvis Presley, The Beatles, and The Beach Boys.

Move over Boomers, Millennials have arrived. Baby Boomers have given birth to the generation, for the first time, that will surpass them. All those Baby Boomers, who are said to be retiring before the decade is up, are topping more than 74 million people in the United States alone, according the latest U.S. Census. It's worth noting, as more younger people immigrate to the U.S., we will continue to see them come together as a society and work to improve their life experiences and ethical behavior.

Generation X

Before moving on to Millennials, we cannot forget to mention Generation X, also referred as the sandwich generation, which is sometimes lost between Baby Boomers and Millennials. This group is savvy and independent. They are also the ones that saw the dot.com bust; they popularized MTV videos and struggled through the AIDS epidemic. This is the generation that rocked its way to Elton John, Queen, Rolling Stones, Fleetwood Mac, and The Jackson Five. Referred to as the "latchkey generation," because they spent part, or most of the day unsupervised or in isolation, when parents were at work, this is a group of individuals who learned to use MTVs videos as a means to communicate. We see a new segue into the type of music as a result. A new sort of phenomena more than just Bebop music, but also Blues and Jazz emerged on the scene.

Moving into the '60s could be best described as a dichotomy with the advent and continuation of "bubble gum" pop on the radio and those younger ones that wanted to express themselves with their own music with a more rocking sound. Now society began to take on a more social conscience with the Vietnam War, which could be seen on TV causing teenagers to question adults and authority.

Millennials (Gen Y)

As of July 2019, the U.S. Census Bureau gave the nod to the Millennial generation as the largest generation in history. This was the result of reasons including the number of deaths and the aging population had been surpassed in size by younger individuals migrating to the U.S.

The Millennial generation is all about information and technology. They are the always-on generation. They have grown-up in a time of unprecedented exponential technological advances that are changing the way we work, live, and play. They have altered every inch of the way we communicate with our friends and family. These young minds understand technology.

They know how to leverage its capabilities and how to advance collaboration, communication, and those within the circle of their community. They are tapping into something even bigger than themselves and they want to make the world better by leveraging all the resources at their fingertips. They feel compelled to apply their vast knowledge to right the wrongs and to fix what's immoral in the world around them and to get their cohorts to join forces. Thus, they are creating a bigger environment and circle of supporters.

In 1987, Strauss and Howe suggested Millennials are people born between 1982 and 2004. These young adults are much better educated than their grandparents and they thrive on innovation. This is the always-on, always connected generation. The fear of not being connected can create a panic in some.

Much to their chagrin and even dismay, this is exactly how the Traditionalists have shaped, encouraged, and molded younger people today. But is this really a bad thing? The younger generation is incredibly talented, committed, and passionate, and that is what gives great promise for humankind.

Watching the challenges and global struggles plaguing previous generations looking through their lens, many

Millennials have the belief they will be the next greatest generation to ever have lived. N.Y. Rep., Alexandria Ocasio-Cortez has already started beating that drum boasting, Millennials are, "Badass." She believes that young people are more informed and dynamic than their predecessors. She says, "They are profoundly courageous because they are willing to puncture taboos and have conversations that frankly older generations struggle to have."

While some might take issue with her sentiments since the Greatest Generation fought to provide the freedom that America has today, Ocasio-Cortez's point is not lost on Millennials who want to improve our global world — one that has seen a lot destruction — by improving the climate and making the world more sustainable.

This is the generation that had to face the realities of the 1999 Columbine High School shooting spree in Littleton Colo., which at that time was the worst high school mass shooting in the U.S. This generation was in high school right before the Great Recession. They struggled with finding a job that was good enough. And, most significantly, they are the generation that felt a sense of duty and joined the military after the World Trade Center Twin Towers collapsed on Sept. 11, 2001, which was truly a defining moment in American history. According to the Department of Defense, more than 1.4 million Millennials joined the military and participated in Iraq and Afghanistan wars.

And despite all the challenges today, Millennials saw the meteoric rise of Mark Zuckerberg's Facebook in 2005 change the world around social media. This generation listened to Michael Jackson, The Cure, Sonic Youth, Madonna, and Bruce Springsteen. It was also during this time period that aging influential rock bands began their "reunion tours" to take advantage of the skyrocketing ticket prices. This is also the time when the "grunge" movement began with bands like Nirvana, Pearl Jam, and Stone Temple Pilots, melding the sounds of punk rock with heavy metal.

Screeners/Gen Z

Gen-X parents have given birth to these "children of crisis." They are also referred to as Generation Z. They are the first generation to be required by the Department of Homeland Security to live at home longer than any other generation in American history. The name was so popular that even Howe found favor in it. In his view, this generation fit it in with the hands-on protective nature of the parenting style of the time and the pandemic.

This is a generation that has grown up immersed in digital technologies. In fact, it would be correct to say they have had a life fully integrated with so many digital devices that it is the norm for communicating from the internet to cellphones, to video games, to any connected device that enhances their digital fluency. The COVID-19 pandemic has also put this generation in front of screens more than ever. And it would be fair to say there has never been a generation that has spent literally most of its time at home in front of digital screens than this generation.

As a generation of crisis, sheltering in place due to COVID-19, perhaps it's more appropriate to refer to them as "Screeners." During the pandemic, a child received little or no supervision for several hours, as parent(s) tried to conduct work in another room of a home behind closed doors. These are children that are spending hours and hours on a screen via a phone, tablet, or computer. This is in contrast to their overprotective parents who were highly active in their lives and paid attention to way too many details.

Generation Z is really the first generation to grow up completely as digital natives. They have experienced the internet as part of their everyday lives. Translation: digital natives expect access to movies and TV shows on demand, high-streaming music, and gaming websites to be instantaneous.

This is a generation that has spent most of their time in front of a computer screen rather than in person. Some estimates suggest this generation could reach as many as two billion globally. This is the disruption generation that is still growing up but already is hooked on instantaneous connections and technology. Simply, as a generation of disruption, they are super comfortable with multiple screens and communicating online. Screeners are passionate about diversity and inclusion and when part of the workforce, wants to work for a company that has the same inclinations. They use technology to solve their most pressing problems. And they believe people and technology can do more to address such things as climate change, social equity, the water crises, and even deforestation.

Screeners/Gen Z will work hard for what they want. They know how to inspire and encourage other members of their younger generation. This is a generation that will be known for struggling to cope with the COVID-19 pandemic.

Music choices for this group are wide and varied. Music has continued its segmentation and although you are not stuck in one segment, one tends to choose a variety that cross over like grunge and punk. Country music has also made a resurgence leading to huge country stars on the music scene. There are also crossover hits from country that now make it into the mainstream music scene. Rap also has found its place growing its fan base as well.

And let's face it, during the COVID-19 pandemic music from Eminem, Coldplay, Kelly Clarkson, Maroon 5, Avril Lavigne, and Kayne West proved instrumental in helping to alter our moods by helping humanity across the globe as we all shelter-in-place.

Cross-Gen Communication

The younger demographic is highly engaged and reachable due to their dependence on social media, and mobile texting. As such they really need to understand the importance of something and how it fits for their overall self-expression. Consider this: most digital natives have created multiple social networks profiles, therefore seeking to engage with diverse voices.

These connections are enhanced by engaging with those whose beliefs and ideas completely mirror those in the inner circle to which they are socially communicating. This plethora of ideas leads to more sharing, less diverse campaigning, greater algorithmic connections, and more ethical and less fractional divisiveness.

They are very tech savvy and have the digital smarts to prove it. They know everything you can think of when it comes to social networking and technology. They know what, where to get it, how to install it, the speed, and some can even program it. They have amassed tremendous knowledge on all things social, pop culture, TV shows, world events, video games, etc. They are the social networking wizards and have it covered.

All of these connections can and have allowed these digital voices to adopt the perspective of each other, proving they are a social force. With technology, users, for instance, can bring racial and ethnic issues to the forefront and openly address inequality, moral, political, and even legal consequences. For the first time, we are seeing this younger generation bring a voice to others who cannot speak for themselves. They recognize the plight of others, those that might not have the same background, or speak the same language.

As such, young consumers have brought more racial and ethnic diversity to American society. This includes leveraging race as a positive social construct and enriching everyone's learning process.

And it is for this reason they feel greater compassion toward individuals and a particular situation that might arise. They are more open to listening to the purpose and the cause that requires their involvement. They seek questions and answers, which ultimately lends credibility to their overall involvement. They need the underlying narrative to ensure fairness. Young adults think about society as a whole and recognize inequality that hurts people's ability to get ahead.

They believe in including everyone and seek to make use of all their tools and knowledge to enable that is happening at all times. Just like Philosopher John Dewey pushed for his progressive movement emphasizing social change, today the focus is also on seeking change through a collaborative approach to enrich everyone's learning process and advocating the richness of and sharing of ideas through better living. Working together, they are able to leverage social sharing and technology advances to communicate an understanding of their vision to create a more sustainable world.

If you wanted to compare a Millennial to a Screener, while you might get the same end result, how the two would approach the task might be slightly different. For instance, Gen Zers are more collaborative and they want to actively engage in changing the way a company works to have more sustainable operations, the livelihood of the brand, and even how they are able to work in that environment to contribute to it. On the other hand, the word activist might describe the way many Millennials will go about achieving the same task.

They would demand change. One is going to watch it, while the other is going to demand it.

Helping Humanity

In the words of author Stephen R. Covey in his book, *The 7 Habits of Highly Effective People,* 2015, "Begin with the end in mind." Today's young people are doing just that. They want to solve problems. Whether they realize it or not, today's young people are here because some 30 years ago innovators were all talking about a personal computer age.

Now we have seen a remarkable transformation, ushering in a new connected global world. With this rapid connected revolution, every aspect of our lives has changed.

The birth of the iPhone (January 2007) opened up peoples' vision to what a smartphone is capable of doing. Now as mobile users, consumers expect smart, connected devices to be lightning-fast, with high-speed web access and to do so much more, and thus this younger generation believes it can do so much more.

Young consumers are demanding more than just the ability to talk from their smartphones. With so many connected devices all around us, these digital natives don't want to waste their time talking on the phone, for most, the preferred method of communication is to text, email, IM (instant message), or use any other form of social media, rather than direct person-to-person communication.

They are instead relying on these devices to manage and move data in the office, in their homes, and even on-the-go to change the world. They want to innovate and transform society to manage and create a biodiversity ecosphere that influences the indigenous people for generations.

As a result of this restoration innovation, they are looking for how to be more engaging, empowering, and regenerative to contribute to a world that has turned grey and muddy. But with instantaneous data and key performance indicators that is changing the definition of what being connected truly means, we have gone well beyond creating innovative gadgets such as tablets, fitness monitors, signage, and home security systems, to ensuring trust and creating new pathways for building and replanting a better tomorrow.

We have yet to imagine what the future will hold as this digital revolution continues to unfold right before our very eyes. Yes, perhaps we can all agree, young people—including those from previous generations—tend to be idealistic. These young people want to change the world for the better. They are demanding that everyone listen. If companies and brands do not get on board quickly, these young professionals will simply find the brands that do. They will buy from the companies that understand.

As already noted, there are differences in the generations—Traditionalists (1925-1942), Baby Boomers (1943-1960), Generation X (1961-1981), Millennials (1982-2004), and Screeners (2005-2019).

One might ask, how can multi-generations come together to address real-world problems that ultimately build on our ability to communicate? Simple is best. So, don't try to overthink the obvious about each generation. To completely understand each generation is to recognize that through the course of history each one struggles with good characteristics and bad attributes, which shapes generational identity. For instance, Millennials are self-identified activists more likely to join rallies focused on issues such as climate change, the #MeToo movement, pay equity, diversity, and immigration. Gen Xers by contrast are less likely to join the streets and these rallies unlike Baby Boomers during their Summer of Love.

There are many differences in how generations adapt to change, apply their technical know-how, and work-to-solve issues of the times including social and economic.

Social Connections

Social media creates a liberating feeling and an interconnectedness that young people enjoy socially across the globe.

Whether it's about staying in the know or communicating with someone they never met face-to-face, they feel they know this individual well who might live thousands of miles away or across a continent. They are influenced by Hollywood elite and they want to be connected to all those influencers.

If there is one common thread among the younger generation it is that they share a common belief in causes. They all want to engage in the effort, and they want to experience new things that are changing the world. They want to give back to their village and to the world around them. They want to be part of vigorous involvement, which includes voluntarism. They believe in supporting the causes they are passionate about and that extends from climate change to the overall environment.

While young people might want to be involved in causes they believe in, where there's good there's always limitations. Let us be noticeably clear, while we have some amazing hope that this younger generation will be the leaders of the Free World, many of the Millennials will also have to really stay actively entrenched to ameliorate the world.

Growing up and entering the world with infinite access to unlimited information, the majority of this generation are born from a generation also referred to as helicopter parents. These are the parents—you know the ingrained stereotypes—who just hover over their children and spoil them forever well into their thirties. These are young adults who think they are entitled.

Some of these high maintenance people, no matter what you do, are never going to get it, because their expectation of themselves is so high because they never had to win anything, they always received a participation trophy.

Most Millennials despise the notion of being considered a digital native, no matter how accurately descriptive the term. However, to call this generation lazy, apathetic, or lacking motivation is only a stereotype hoisted upon them.

This is an activist-ready generation that simply needs to be motivated. Inspiration for this new wave of socialization is not given through a career, per se, but by core beliefs.

This generation is generally defined as passionate and looking to better the world by leveraging innovation and using it as a source of strength to overcome the world's biggest challenges. If, however, a job is in sync with how they view their personal happiness then they can make the world a better place, and the outcome will be productive.

They seek to thwart environmental divisiveness. They see no ethnic boundaries and they strive to build a better global community. The younger generation wants to rise up and move this country forward just like their grandparents.

This generation has faced challenges and if they can align their job with those goals of work, environment, and future generations, they see it as victory for everyone.

Paycheck vs. Passion

This is a generation that wants to galvanize in consistent and ongoing volunteerism. Too often their needs are not properly understood. They demand to have their voices heard. They engage with protestors to think about big issues around the environment, climate change, circular economy, water shortages, destruction of the forest, and the indigenous people. If they can lift their collective voices, they believe they can build their social capital, expand their networks, and contribute to society in an excessively big way.

As one member of this generation put it, when we understand the traits of the younger generations, we can make the most of our interactions with them and we can come together multigenerational to solve any problem. They have the ability to strengthen their communities from the inside.

These insights and suggestions are valuable not just for solving environmental issues, but helping any political party looking to extend its view.

Young people want to believe and participate in something bigger than themselves. They want to make money to fund their lifestyle, sure, but they also want to give back and be part of something unique, special, and important — like themselves. They need to connect to something worthwhile, meaningful, or something cool. They want to see that light at the end of the tunnel. Something bigger than themselves.

Interestingly, younger members of the generation differ slightly from their older counterparts in that they have a stronger motivation to achieve economic security. We are understanding how to interact with younger team members, which means as a society we can overcome literally all political, economic, and environmental hurdles put in front of corporate America.

With the right determination in policies, workers can solve technical and business challenges. Imagine the breakthrough in communication to anyone that engages with younger generations and the barriers that are overcome. And if you are part of the younger generation, perhaps these observations will help you understand how to develop your strengths and overcome struggles in all these contexts, especially looking at environmental potential.

Simply, five generations can solve any crisis and conquer any nation. As we discussed earlier, the younger generation prefers group interactions to one-to-one interactions, so they work well in team-oriented situations. They thrive in a brainstorming and in ideation-sharing environments where they can contribute to the direction and outcomes of the group. Each has their own unique approach and takes great pride in being part of a team that supports their efforts. They want to contribute their individuality to that winning team.

This gives them an opportunity to place their unique, special, and important seal on the team success of the project.

Work and Play

Young employees are loyal to several ideals that can range from individuality, creativity, and educational environments that push their company's success. They are the ones that focus of the social economics. They have an eye on the big global picture. If the goal is to activate young people, the objective needs to be to connect with them on the reasoning behind every—and all corporate decisions—and how those decisions impact the environment.

They want to understand economic inclusion, opportunity for building and hiring locally, with a keen focus on diversity. Younger workers want to know that employers do what they say and implement it into daily functions for carbon reduction, circularity, and green. The shift in the workforce is not about the long hours. No longer is this about getting people to work for decades. This generation wants to do more and for more.

They are socially conscious and environmentally responsible. They have the will and a great desire to change the world through a life well lived and experiences they have enjoyed.

Many young people are labeled entitled, which often leads them to being in direct conflict with older generations. It is this lack of understanding which widens the gap and leads to greater vitriol among some of the younger generation. Understanding the desire and passion of young people will help employers looking for ways to recruit, retain, and inspire the next generation of corporate leaders. Much of this has to do with explaining and not telling. The younger generation is all about diversity, and they question authority that do not understand expression of choice.

In his book, *Answering Why,* Mark C. Perna, 2018, made the point that passion has to come from within the young person, born of personal desire and aspirations. Passion also comes from knowing where you are going and why you are going there, building confidence and doing it successfully, learning what it takes to succeed, and then heading in the right direction. The resulting passion creates confidence and the resolve and determination to see their plan through over the long run.

In the Christian faith it has been taught for years: time, talent, and treasures. The church encourages the faithful to get involved as their personal pathway to provide and to help everyone. This is generally the same idea within a company when creating a sustainability action plan for a company. But now, each team is building and creating a plan that works for a company that can achieve the desired success within the organization and then carry it on outside the four walls through the supply chain, to the jobsite, to the distribution channel into the circular economy. In the end, it is about building upon the successes again, again, and again.

We are no longer telling our younger workers how to do things; they are inspiring all of us and teaching the world how to be more effective, efficient, and less wasteful. Parents would tell their children not to waste, to turn off the lights, and how to be more economical. From a spiritual perspective, giving back to God what God has given back to you. Many people have learned the three T's of giving of time, talent, and tithing (treasure). We have been given gifts and how we choose the use them is what is key.

With greater focus on efficiency and improving our education, today's younger generation is creating a more desired global lifestyle so that everyone can live healthier and more sustainable lives. We need creative minds to solve global sustainable problems.

As we have been saying for years, there are millions of jobs available, but millions of people out of work. This means companies need to reconsider their views on who they hire and what positions they are filling. This means management needs to change its views about who we hire to run our manufacturing, retail, distribution, supply chains, and so much more.

Millennials are influencing brands daily. Retailers and manufacturers recognize the intense influence that this generation has in their purchasing power as they use multiple devices a day to influence their buying decision.

Michael Walton, manufacturing industry executive, Microsoft, admits Millennials have a sense of loyalty to a specific retail brand and how passionate they are to that brand and that brand's suite of products. He says he is seeing that translate into their roles at manufacturers and their job, really forcing that change. And the good news is he says almost every customer he works with has a sustainability report. And sustainability, more importantly, ranks as one of the top five most important items on a CEO's horizon.

He adds, when manufacturers and retailers are forward thinking in their planning, it is not just, does it save us money? How do we fund it? It is a demand. No longer is it just an option on the table. He says Millennials demanded it through their purchase power and their passion around certain specific topics.

Millennials are willing to share their thoughts and opinions on the platform. Millennials are more loyal to authenticity than an ad. Ads don't just work for them.

Simply, the digital marketing must create and send the right content messages to omnichannels. Examples today include digital marketing, search engine optimization, social media, and email marketing. E-commerce aggressively pursues omnichannel strategies that blend e-commerce with traditional commerce in a way that puts every customers' needs first.

This means addressing purchase power from offline to online and considering online marketplaces (Amazon and Groupon) to even addressing major individual brands (Under Armour and adidas).

Millennials speak from their heart. They are eager to dominate the social media message. This generation of leaders expect brands to speak to them directly one-on-one or through social media with as many content delivery methods as possible. That means companies have to step up their game to develop strong, emotionally driven relationships that impact buying decisions. These are the consumers that are making decisions about brands. They want to dominate culture, impart new passion on reviving our ecosystem, and change the modern world for future generations to come.

Keeping all of these factors in mind and building on Howe's original catalyst of the Fourth Turning, I predict the next 10 years will be important for how we address sustainability, climate, and the circular economy.

CHAPTER 2

HISTORY

History

It's hard to really grasp the magnitude of the confluence of forces that are creating this incredible disruption. But let's examine the change that is impacting the world around us.

Through rapid increased connectivity and instant access to data, we are seeing user rate of acceptance increase exponentially, in contrast to past invention, which took much longer for adoption. The telephone, for instance, was invented in 1876, but it actually took almost a century for landlines to reach a saturation point in consumer households. Looking at the numbers, by all accounts, it actually took some 39 years for telephones to gain enough traction to reach about 40% penetration and another 15 years before we saw them become ubiquitous. Smartphones, on the other hand, accomplished a 40% penetration rate in just 10 years.

Most can agree we are experiencing the greatest metamorphosis in history, possibly since the Industrial Revolution. Perhaps the greatest and most significant impact since the adoption of machines is the Information Revolution. While some might disagree, history will ultimately tell the tale. However, based on the speed and breadth, the Information Revolution will have an even greater influence on the use of machines and how information will be extrapolated and applied to run our companies better than the influence of machines in our past.

During the Industrial Revolution, technological changes appeared on the scene slowly. Innovations often met with strong resistance from state officials and other guilds concerned that technologies would replace entire industries of trades people. But by 1700 in England, and by 1750 in France, the resistance to change had weakened, signaling the winds of change and technology adoption was quickly taking flight. By the beginning of the 18th century, machines were used extensively in manufacturing, which revolutionized the way products could be produced.

We are also experiencing a rapid acceleration in the scope, scale, adoption, and economic impact of technology. Look at it this way, technological progress has surpassed anything we could have imagined, and not only is the speed of technology advancing, but so is consumer adoption. We have the infrastructure to embrace the technology and generation after generation is accepting technological advances in every form and shape in their personal and professional lives, faster than investors can imagine them.

Today, however, we are witnessing the adoption of home appliances, cellphones, smartphones, social media, tablets, computers, health devices, and just about any connected device or thing you can think of in the modern era. It's all about instantaneous information at our fingertips. In 2020, according to Global System for Mobile Communications Association (GSMA), the worldwide number of smartphone owners reached 3.5 billion people, which simply translates to 44.81% users globally. With almost half of the world connected in one form or another, that is proving there are fewer barriers to entry.

What's perhaps most significant is to think the first-generation iPhone was finally released to the public for purchase in June 2007. Since that time, the impact that connected devices has made across the world has been remarkable. Just a mere three years after its launch, developers had already created some 153,000 applications. By 2020, the market embraced more than two million iOS applications and for Android devices just shy of three million. With the aforementioned mobile app usage data, we can then estimate that millions of apps are downloaded across the globe every day.

From iPhone to Tablet

No one could have imagined at the time how big of an impact that one device would have on both our personal and professional lives. Since its original launch, the Apple iPad has also experienced very impressive growth.

It should be noted American computer scientist Alan Kay first imagined a tablet-computer world for children. Although he might have been ahead of his time, he had outlined the DynaBook concept in a 1972 paper, publishing the benefits of a personal computer device for children, while working on Xerox PARC. His masterful imagination saw the future of tablets weighing less than 4-lbs., the size of an average notebook, at a cost of only $500. He also suggested a 4/C display, a stylus, and even voice. Does all this sound familiar today? Again, this was all written in the early '70s long before Steve Jobs introduced the Apple iPad and before laptops had been invented.

While Kay might have imagined a world of personal computer devices when it came to size, scope, processor, and power, the world itself was not ready for all the technological advances he was writing about just yet. Apple, on the other hand, saw the future, and developed its own iPad tablet— when the technology and market was ready in April 2010. And today, if you look at the overall numbers, tablet computers continue to gain in popularity because consumers can browse the internet, connect to social network apps, display HD videos, and used for video conferencing (which was even greater due to the pandemic).

Amazon Effect

Whether you agree with the premise or not, we are all witnessing a not so quiet revolution that affects every person: The Amazon Effect. That is a fact that is incontrovertible.

Amazon has changed our view of same day shipping, robotic warehouses, and artificial intelligence applied to customer decision-making and is collectively having a massive disruptive impact on the supply chain. Simply, for any market Amazon has entered, it has either galvanized action among its competitors, forced them either out of business, or certainly to rethink how they do business online.

There has been a transition from the early days of eCommerce ("e" for "electronic"), to mCommerce ("m" is for "mobile") and on to what is known as omnichannel commerce. As each of these came into prominence, interrelating devices and applications expanded, as consumers we embraced buying behaviors to tap our potential. Now, what we have all witnessed is an impressive shift away from traditional "ship to stores" fulfillment practices to "ship direct" requirements.

This has dramatically accelerated order volume growth and fulfillment delivery expectations far beyond the structural and human resource capabilities of traditional retailers. Amazon has taken charge leading eCommerce retailers and its revolution with an unwavering commitment to relentless improvements on how and when an order is delivered to consumers.

Putting things in context, Amazon began in 1995. At that time, the internet was just 26 years old—it started as the ARPANET (Advanced Research Projects Agency Network) in 1969, the year we first landed on the moon. The World Wide

Web, founded in 1989 (the "www" in a URL web address), was just about six years old in 1995.

Telecoms began making a comeback with the start of mCommerce, the access to the internet through smartphones and other smart devices like tablets. In fact, actually pegged as the first smartphone because BellSouth Cellular Corp., had managed to put a computer inside of a phone, officially called, Simon. Simon was a hybrid wireless device that could be used as a telephone, pager, electronic mail service, address book, calendar, and fax machine. Featuring a touchscreen (stylus required) and weighing in at a little more than a pound, Simon sold for $899 in 1994.

So, by 1997, smartphones, with application capabilities, started to gain some excitement. But as we all know, the real traction emerged with the introduction of Apple's iPhone in 2007. This was the seminal event for the explosion of mCommerce in the U.S. As in Asia, smartphones had been in use from the late 1990s, but the real explosion and enthusiasm came with consumers standing in lines to purchase an Apple device, which gave all of them the ability to browse the web just as they would from a desktop computer–with a tap of a finger.

Consumers all over the world yearned for this new device and Amazon worked behind the scenes building on the needs and wants of buyers alike. Today there is no question that Amazon leads the race as the most popular shopping app, only trailed by Walmart in the United States with a projected 200 million mobile users by 2025.

Hello Prime

mCommerce gives consumers the ability to scan product codes while in a retailer's store, find a link to it, and then shop for the best price and delivery option. This is where Amazon, with its relentless push to accelerate order fulfillment, delivery time, and with the introduction of Prime, eliminated the last two barriers to making a purchase in the store a better option: Sales taxes and delivery charges. Prime didn't just knock down barriers, it ran them over like a bulldozer. But that all changed in April 2017, when it was required to collect sales taxes in the first of five states and then shortly thereafter that changed and it collected taxes from 45 states in total and Washington, D.C.

This capability to shop for an alternative supplier while standing in a retail store or simply in a home is known as: showrooming or webrooming. Coupled with the viral word of mouth capabilities of the social networks or being able to call a friend and instantly tell them that they are able to achieve a better deal from "X" rather than make the drive to a specific store location. These are the results of today's mighty online consumer shopping habits. With the game-changing Amazon Prime scenario, consumers pay an annual fee to be guaranteed one and two-day service shipping for tens of millions of products. Amazon constantly looks to stay ahead of the pack and has once again upped the ante only recently, offering customers a two-hour delivering service.

Consumer behavior like showrooming played a key role in changing the retail business model. Traditional retailing gave control to the retailer because the purchaser had to walk through the door of a retail store to purchase the product. The timing for merchandise displays, pricing, and demand-driving discounting gave retailers control over the brands they were selling. Today brand control has shifted in a big way.

PCs and smartphones altered the complexity. Brands now had the freedom to communicate and engage directly with the consumer. Unlike in the past, brands had the flexibility to offer their own enticing value propositions, and while in the early days, eCommerce would not directly fulfill the orders, it would have the ability to guide a consumer to a specific retailer, offering most favorable positioning and promotion to the brand. 'Oh the good ole days;' is what many retailers echoed long before Amazon entered the scene and put many brick and mortar retailers out of business.

mCommerce further disrupted the traditional model: The freedom to shop anywhere and at any time through a smartphone put both the brands and retailers on notice. And again, along came Amazon with its experimentation around same day delivery.

Think about this for a moment using a different kind of retail experience: Food shopping. The first same day online ordering and delivery service for food was Webvan. Webvan was a dot.com company and grocery business that filed for bankruptcy in 2001 after a measly three years in business. Fast forward to today, and there are now a host of successful startups (including Amazon's) that are growing at phenomenal rates.

The difference: In 2001, the traditional food industry fulfillment center was oriented to "ship to stores" methodologies, and the cost of operating a same day, rapid delivery business such as Webvan tried—so fundamentally different in its order fulfillment requirements than those supporting daily shipments to brick and mortar stores—devastated the profitability of the business model.

Let's try to unpack all of this a little bit. First, even before COVID-19 had the world all sheltering-in-place, online food services like DoorDash, GrubHub, and Uber Eats accounted for almost 80% of the sector revenue. There are many others that account for the remainder of the market. In fact, Waiter.com, which unveiled in 1995 as World Wide Waiter, still exists and delivers today. Perhaps the best way to look at any food delivery services, after comparing price, is fast, hot, and the one that gets your food safely to your doorstep. While every generation since the pandemic has now taken advantage of these subscription food services, there is no doubt the socially engaged generation have mastered even having McDonald's delivered.

That is why other types of grocery delivery services have felt increased competition. Peapod, which launched in October 1989, has led the market. Since its launch, the Chicago-based company has seen increased competition from the likes of Amazon and Instacart.

Showrooming

Showrooming actually turned the retail business model upside down. Traditional retailing gave control to the retailer because you had to come to the store to buy what you wanted. In the past, customer service was an ideal trump card for exceptional retailers. However, now they are in the midst of a mobile revolution.

Brands and retailers recognize smartphones give incredible power to customers to make essential purchases. Unlike in the past, they have new methods of customer engagement to capture and entice new and existing customers. Thus, the rise of omnichannel or multichannel commerce has made its way into our culture and is here to stay. Engaging with the customer from initial point of contact means understanding how he or she researches a product to the actual final purchases through any venue, including online, smartphone, web, or at the store.

As the expectations of actual demands of customers has risen to what they want as fast and as cheaply as possible have risen exponentially, so has the disconnect between traditional order fulfillment and rapid response fulfillment operations in distribution centers.

Sadly, we have seen the Great Awakening, sometimes a brutal one, among brands and retailers, as the shift from ship to store-fulfillment is replaced by "ship direct." (These awakenings similar to the seasons that Howe references.

Success now all depends on marketing and direct innovation and delivery rather than on pure production.

Innovation in technology is rapidly eroding barriers of space and time and is changing the way customers interact with retail brands and how they respond to those brands. This is all corresponding with the rapid increase of smaller orders that are going right out the door (to prevent angering a customer who, as industry statistics show, will not place a future order as a result of the bad experience). The customer is always right!

Just a few short years ago, if consumers were to visit a typical retailer's distribution center, they would see racks stretching from floor to ceiling jammed with full cases of products. Aisle after aisle for hundreds of feet. Workers on forklifts would scurry about, stopping at a particular location, jumping off the lift, and pulling a couple of cases onto the wooden pallet held by the lift.

A logistics worker would continue to do this, building pallet upon pallet that would be staged in a location near a loading door. At one point during the process, trucks would be loaded at the docks. Every truck would have one or more stops at individual stores, where the pallets would be delivered, and retail workers would restock the store shelves in anticipation of next day's retail delivery of goods. Yes. This was a typical "ship to store" model for many, many decades — and it worked.

What eCommerce and mCommerce have forced on retailers is an entirely different order fulfillment process that they are now struggling to accommodate. There is no doubt we are living in an age when consumers are demanding quicker service, greater personalization, and a speed to market that is unparalleled to anything we have ever seen previously.

Change isn't easy. Historically, the supply chain was the last place scarce capital was allocated. However, dramatic change has occurred and it is being led by Amazon leader Jeff Bezos.

Ship It My Way

Twenty years ago, order fulfillment in distribution centers was a paper-based process. It wasn't unusual to see a day's worth of orders for an entire company's retail stores to be printed on paper. Logistics supervisors would sort the work by truck to determine the best route which and stores to visit on the list. These sorted and batched orders would then be handed to selectors, who would head their forklifts to the aisle. In a way, Amazon's solution is a departure from the effort to "automate" human performance in distribution centers in the past 20 years. Back then most order fulfillment processing was focused on shipping products to brick-and-mortar stores where customers went to purchase them. When Amazon went online in 1995, the era of direct-to-consumer fulfillment got underway. Selectors determined how best to go from location to location to grab the products listed on the orders.

As competitive pressures began mounting, the "follow my own selection path" methodology that gave selectors complete control of the path they would follow and the time they would take to complete an order was recognized to be even more inefficient. Around this time, also, a new technology was introduced to better control inventory management. This was the barcode, and with it came the requirement for connected, smart, wireless devices necessary to scan the codes.

With barcode scanning, and the evolutionary leap forward in IT systems designed to manage its complexity, order selection became more "directed" and less under the control of the human selectors. It allowed for specific, system-assigned "pick paths" to be given to selectors, and with the increased data collection capabilities of the devices and supporting software, the first big improvement in productivity measurement was now underway.

Companies are now able to measure each human selector's performance time, compare one to many, and allow for the imposition of performance standards. With performance standards we now have increased incentive programs. This means the birth of the selectors are being offered the carrot of incentive bonuses to beat the standard but were heavily penalized if they consistently dropped below that same standard. Order selection by scanning created the first technology-based augmentation of human productivity for distribution.

Today, the highest levels of technology-enhanced human performance in distribution centers come from the use of voice-driven selection and "pick to light" techniques. Both of these focus on minimizing the need for the human selector to think about what someone is doing. Rather, the continuous prompting of next step after next step drives the selector to continuously move as instructed. In all cases, the human selector is moving from one location to the next, down a path that has been predetermined by software algorithms and delivered by wireless devices.

It's no wonder then how Amazon has changed the dynamics of the selection process. It recognized that having a human move from location to location, stop, select, and validate products, and repeat this process hundreds of times a day, was extremely inefficient. Amazon has simply proven that a fleet of robots, operating in a "human exclusion zone," can bring entire shelves of products to the human standing in a fixed location much faster. Amazon got rid of "the walk" in its eighth-generation fulfillment center.

The increase in order fulfillment productivity has been staggering. It has also been fundamental to Amazon's drive to provide same day delivery. If a fulfillment center can now fulfill a customer order within 15 minutes from when the "buy" button was pushed by a customer, then the ability to deliver that day with the transportation options now available, it becomes not just a reality, but a service commitment.

This is a fundamental change in how productivity growth will be measured and leveraged. Couple that with a new paradigm shift, as robots become cheaper and more capable. They will move from their traditional roles on factory floors into new industries. Collaborative robots are being integrated into more types of environments and performing more varied tasks—from stocking shelves and assisting factory workers to performing services in the home. Their ascendancy into the factory floors and into new industries is significant as next-generation leaders see what they can do.

This rapid transformation that we are all witnessing therefore is predicated by a profound realization. A sagacity that is being driven by the younger generation who have made it painfully obvious that the linear take-make-waste model can longer exist. Simply, it has been a colossal failure for the environment. The emerging model is being replaced by what is referred to as a circular economy and a more sustainable world. As described by the United Nations, that has to do with meeting the needs of the present without compromising the ability of the future generations to meet their needs.

CHAPTER 3

CIRCULAR

This is our one opportunity to turn to the young innovators for help. They want to help; and we need to give them a shot to design and restore our natural ecosystems: our forests, soils, clean water, clean energy, and clean air. They have the experience and passion, and we must trust them to secure our world. – **Peggy Smedley**

A Throwaway Economy

In 1966, Kenneth Boulding made a bold prediction on the environment and the economy in his essay, *"The Economics of the Coming Spaceship Earth."* His vision at the time recognized the ability to be a more sustainable economy and require humankind to step back and reevaluate how we view ourselves alongside of nature, production, and consumption, completely differently than we had previously.

While Boulding's essay only touches the surface, his thoughts might have ignited many of today's environmental leaders' expansive visions for sustainability, circularity, and green discussions.

For the sake of this discussion, let's acknowledge that manufacturers planned to build obsolescence into their own factory assembly lines and the products they were distributing to every consumer, starting with the Industrial Revolution. The reason was they either didn't know or didn't care during that period. In either case, it happened.

In recent decades, we have amassed all this stuff and it has just piled up in one landfill after another. At this point, the direction of its flow (like carbon in the atmosphere), and plastic in the ocean) has been drawing considerable concern. And the more we have been taking away from our natural resources, the more companies, governments, and individuals are starting to talk about being green.

The take-make-waste model was successful for many decades. We saw many highly productive manufacturing factories prosper. Many factories proved plentiful as take and make systems. As humans we became comfortable with things, and making more things, and then more things. So much so, we became known as the throw-it-away society.

And words like circular economy, sustainability, and climate change all become part of the everyday nomenclature.

The Ellen MacArthur Foundation, says a circular economy is based on the principles of designing out waste and pollution, keeping products and materials in use, and regenerating natural systems. Simply, we are talking about being more restorative by design, which is having profound implications on business, economics, and governments.

Today, this linear economy of take-make-waste, where we see material flow directly from resource extraction through manufacturing processes to landfills has reached its capacity. More specifically, environmentalists point to unsustainable assembly that depletes natural resources and consistently pollutes the environment. While the goal of a circular economy is based on reducing the load, reuses, and redeveloping resources through a renewable process.

We are hearing over and over again we are on the precipice of failure unless we act now. We are within a decade of pure carbon collapse unless we heed the global warnings of the scientists. And what's more, the United States is the second largest culprit of CO_2 emissions, trailing only to China.

According to the Circularity Gap Report, the upward trend in resource extraction and greenhouse gas emissions still flows in the wrong direction. Simply meaning it is only at 8.6% circular. And that means the gap is not narrowing. Interestingly, two years ago it was at 9.1% circular. Things are clearly going in the wrong direction. No surprise there when you think about how we consume things in this world. So, guess what? There is a lot of work to be done, especially if there's any hope of achieving climate change and reducing the current levels of 1.5 °C (2.7 °F). Perhaps the bigger question is whether we can even consider reaching the aforementioned goals if we can't get individuals, companies, and countries all on the same page?

The Intergovernmental Panel on Climate Change (IPCC), the UN's body for assessing pre-industrial climate change and GHG, coupled with human-induced warming, revealed that confidence is very unlikely based on existing global patterns.

However, the IPCC has shed some light on the idea that if countries truly invested in an all-out effort to drastically focus on reducing CO_2 emissions, as a result of leveraging human communities committed across all economies and countries, it would drastically reveal environmental improvements. These global efforts would alter the interconnectivity of the past, present, and future adaptation and human-environment and sustainable development.

Sometimes that means thinking beyond what we can envision today for our communities and cities. Sustainable Design Manager, Monica Miller Brown, noted that's exactly what Thyssenkrupp Elevator does when it designs its elevators, thinking about a sustainable and circular economy today.

She explained that most people struggle with the idea of closing the loop, but that's where the 20-year-old lift company excels in ferrying tenants in style to the upper floors. When Thyssenkrupp Elevator puts a product in the world, Miller Brown noted that its mission is to maintain it for the rest of its life. If the moveable room comes to the end of its use, she emphasized how the company dispatches efficiency and sustainability in the building process by touching the elevator from cradle to reuse. Thereby proving that circularity through reuse or through reuse or extended lifespan has its place even for large integral building products.

Here's a known fact: the first global warming prediction was made as far back in 1896. It was actually made when Svante Arrhenius had estimated the burning of fossil fuels would eventually release enough CO_2 to warm the Earth by 5 °C. The fundamental physics underlying the calculations has not changed, according to scientists, but not surprisingly, predictions on the other hand are all over the place when it comes to really putting a finger on what exactly the future holds.

We will get into a greater discussion on the Paris Agreement in the next chapter. But for now, let's acknowledge the Paris Agreement's underlying objective is not without merit — global collaboration, social justice, and systemic change. The goal of getting all countries to set a low-carbon agenda for all world countries to be supportive and complementary is lofty and worthwhile, but is it reasonable in a world where global leaders march to the beat of their own drum when it comes to pollution and building coal plants, and the like?

To understand the circular economy, we need to focus on less pollution, which means having a low-carbon agenda. We all need to be collaborating across all countries. We need to be mutually supportive: the right fit at the right price.

Companies need to transition to circularity. That means thinking about circular economy strategies. With the right goals, companies will not only reduce waste, but they will make money. Just shy of 30% of organizations admit to implementing some type of circular design approaches into their systems. That means technology is playing a role, but the opportunity for companies to continue their journey of reinvention will continue for the next decade. These new circular business models and improved resource efficiencies should open more opportunities for a restorative and regenerative economy that potentially could generate as much as $4.5 trillion by 2030.

Unlike the previously mentioned take-make-waste linear model, the Ellen MacArthur Foundation defines a circular economy based on the principle of designing out waste and pollution in favor of keeping products and materials in use, and regenerating nature systems.

Each time we discard our food waste to rot away, we contribute even more methane emissions being released into the atmosphere. According the U.S. EPA, landfill gases comprise almost 18% of U.S. methane emissions, which is the equivalent of 103 million metric tonnes of CO_2 released in the atmosphere.

Take a look at the food fight debate. We know that nearly one third of all food is lost or wasted globally, an estimated 1.3 billion tonnes each year, according to the Food and Agriculture (FAO) of the United Nations. Couple this with the fact that at the same time we are letting almost a billion people go hungry.

Prior to COVID-19, the FAO projected 80% of all food would be consumed in cities by 2050. Whether that estimate will still ring true is anyone's guess. The more important point here is that urban and rural food growers need to put greater emphasis on the value of their food production and consider better sustainability methods. By making food circularity a top priority they can grow efforts to improve health benefits for its community well into the future.

Rather than waste all this food, it can be redistributed to help feed the most vulnerable. To put this problem in a more visual perspective the numbers speak for themselves. Here's something to think about; every second edible food is not harvested, and it gets spilled or otherwise lost or wasted it is the equivalent of six garbage trucks.

Currently less than 2% of cities have made the commitment to reduce food waste through composting, or the reclaiming of organic material. There is a lot of work to be done to promote healthier bacteria that break down organic matter and reduce the overall waste impact. While this might not address all the hunger problems, it will go a long way to feeding the people who need it most.

We are wasting too much food. We need to solve this crisis and inspire the next generation to be innovative. Many universities and colleges, high schools, and middle schools have engaged in programs that encourage competitions and recycle mania efforts, all of which are great efforts, but it's still not enough. We need sustainable homes, work, campuses, communities, and everything in between. We need more than a village. We need Planet Earth.

Case Study

Going Up

Elevators have been in buildings for hundreds of years. They have even found their way into some of the most elaborate of homes and into the highest peaks in the world. As these vertical transport capabilities get more sophisticated, they are showing up at some of the most unimaginable heights.

There was a time when people referenced these movable rooms as cage lifts from the depths of coal mines; to rollercoasters, tram-like elevators, and even robots, and with the pandemic we have seen the rise of touchless solutions and kick-button solutions. The point is elevators are changing faster today than they have in 100 years previously.

Sustainable Design Manager, Monica Miller Brown, at Thyssenkrupp Elevator admitted that most people struggle with the idea of closing the loop when it comes to talking about circularity and sustainability. For instance, traction elevator systems are equipped with an energy recovery function that allow for energy generated by braking to be put back into the building's power grid.

This energy regeneration can account for up to 50% of the energy used by the elevator itself. The company understands that efficient vertical transportation is critical to efficient land use and sensitivity to the environment and society.

Thyssenkrupp Elevator has committed to a set of environmental goals that include operational use of an innovative smart-routing system to optimize use and reduce energy consumption. The TWIN elevator system, or two elevators in one hoistway, was debuted by Thyssenkrupp Elevator in 2018 in the U.S. This can reduce the floor area used by elevators in half, increasing the floor area ratio and density of a neighborhood, protecting undeveloped land.

Thyssenkrupp Elevator has adapted its business strategies to address sustainability, reducing material environmental, social, governance (ESG) impacts on its products and closing the loop by maintaining the elevator until end-of-life usage. Miller Brown affirmed that as the elevator comes to the end of its use, Thyssenkrupp Elevator dispatches efficiency and sustainability in the building industry by renovating any and all parts of the elevator from cradle to reuse.

The company has proven that refurbishing older elevators can lower its energy consumption by up to 70% and extends an elevator's use phase by an additional 25 years. The global indication is clear as circularity has its place for these solutions. Mitigation and adaptation reduce carbon and restore efficiency to the building's operation.

Another sustainability innovation was the introduction of double-deck elevators in 2008 at the Shanghai World Financial Center, China's tallest building. Smart, sustainable buildings use centralized, intelligent energy control systems that are often combined with solar panels, geothermal wells, harvested rainwater, natural lighting, and other environmentally friendly techniques to significantly lower energy usage.

One option for greater energy efficiency for people moving is the MULTI elevator system. This ropeless elevator is capable of vertical and horizontal movement using linear motors, which is proving that elevators can actually change beyond the traditional cab systems. The MULTI, transport capacities can be increased by up to 50%, and peak energy consumption can be cut by 60% when compared to whole conventional elevator systems. Skybridges are being adopted in more towers around the world especially when combined with other smart, connected, and sustainable global materiality impacts.

Miller Brown finds herself training other Thyssenkrupp Elevator employees on circularity because it's still a new buzzword. With sustainability and circularity, Thyssenkrupp Elevator is always trying to keep pace with customer demand and its key pillars to reduce emissions. That means taking care of customers and helping them choose the right product at all times. And maybe that means alternative solutions in an effort to maintain customers for decades to come. Ultimately, by doing that, Thyssenkrupp Elevator is demonstrating how the circular perspective will continue to grow to become part of everyone's vocabulary.

For instance, Thyssenkrupp Elevator management knew it had to create a solution that was fully environmentally friendly, as the elevator market was changing, but at the same time, it needed a sustainable solution for the surge in urban population. While other elevator companies were pivoting away from hydraulic systems that are the workhorse of the industry, Thyssenkrupp Elevator was developing a hydraulic oil specifically for elevators that's 99% canola based.

With a bio-based fluid, Thyssenkrupp Elevator has eliminated environmental concerns and gives its customers a solution that has the full circular economy idea that for a low-rise, low-use application will cost them less to maintain and operate. Ultimately, Miller Brown explained the company wants to make the right product for the right buildings so that it will remain in the building longer and extend the lifecycle of the product to at least 25 years if not longer.

She admitted Thyssenkrupp Elevator still has work to do, of course, to be a more sustainable company, but it is making good progress in serving its customers. Miller Brown punctuated the point with this example. Elevators are made up of mostly steel, which is nearly 75% recycled content and also highly recyclable. Elevators can be updated to maintain a lifespan of nearly 25 years. At the end of its life much of the product gets recycled and remade into steel for new elevators. Circuit boards and other fewer recyclable products are remanufactured for similar elevators still in use and serviced by Thyssenkrupp Elevator.

More work is being done to enhance its lightweight nature and to extend its life span as well as to further its environmentally friendly way to move people efficiently.

How Did We Pollute the Earth?

Even before the Industrial Revolution, there were fewer people, less pollution, and natural resources were abundant. The Industrial Revolution—which began in England in the 18th century, before impacting neighboring countries France and Germany—made its way across the Atlantic Ocean to the United States. What do we know? Man was overly eager to achieve incredible production that was profitable and efficient. Were there ecological consequences of taking endless supply of resources from Mother Earth? Did anyone consider the ramifications for future generations on the environment and the ecosystem degradation that would arise from depleting natural resources?

Artisan guild factories proved highly efficient for their time supporting hundreds of workers; providing them with the power and machinery needed for incredible productivity. In 1762, Matthew Boulton began constructing a remarkable factory capable of employing more than 600 people working lathes, alongside polishing, and grinding machines powered by a very impressive steam engine. Thomas Newcomen is on record as designing the first steam engine in 1705, only to be improved upon by James Watt in 1763, all of which created an epochal shift to the extent work could be performed in a plant.

The steam engine had an effect on the geographical landscape. Liberated from water, it was possible to build factories and ultimately industrial cities away from running water. It was also possible to put power sources on mobile assets such as Robert Fulton's experimental steam vessel Clermont that sailed the Hudson in 1807.

Perhaps it was the Embargo Act of 1807 (prohibited American merchant ships from leaving foreign ports and prohibited foreign vessels from carrying American goods out of American ports) that set the wheels in motion and forced Americans to make their own goods purely out of survival.

It was this instinct that led them to focus heavily on advancing factory technology so quickly, leaving humankind unable to resist the excitement of the manufacturing age that brought with its limitless ideas for the expansion of the industrial era. This was the beginning of artisans—makers of hand-made products—being replaced by machines.

Roads, bridges, and railroads began to be sprawled across the United States and other parts of the world. Names like Andrew Carnegie (coal), John D. Rockefeller (oil), Cornelius Vanderbilt (railroads/steel), and Henry Ford (automobiles) had made themselves known, and rich, but had changed the course of history forever.

As time progressed, more and more goods were manufactured and continued to play an integral role in this production. The next major change in manufacturing came at the conclusion of the First World War. After World War I, Henry Ford and General Motors' Alfred Sloan, transformed manufacturing from what had been known as craft production into the age of mass production.

His pioneering efforts revealed that mass producers were able to fabricate standardized products in very-high volume. Pioneered in 1913, Ford's mass production system produced the famous Model T, and propelled the auto industry and a host of other industries throughout the world. Now more goods were being produced in factories and assembly lines were humming louder and faster than ever. Life was good. But was it?

This broken linear system goes only one way from producer directly to consumer to the trash bin. Nothing goes back to nature. What was designed, built, and sold was soon replaced. And the old item would eventually find its way into a trash graveyard.

Environmental Carnage

Businesses continued to flourish. Little or no regulation was managing the environmental damage that was creating havoc on Mother Earth. Demand for coal made the mining industry exceedingly popular. Even the use of mass production and electricity was taking its toll on the power grid.

These amazing small-scale factories got bigger. These factories became full-blown mass producers of products and without any government regulation. Their pollutants had no regard for the disposal of waste, recycling, or let alone knowing how to discard the dangerous contaminants they were generating.

Consumers enjoyed these new finished goods that factories started to produce in mass. This was big business. The business landscape was being transformed and companies started to revolutionize industry. The more industry grew, the world witnessed the rise of the industrialization. The bigger the manufacturing plant, the greater the concern. Somewhere along the way, we started to realize our planet just couldn't keep up with the exhausting and ever-increasing demands.

Much of our overconsumption and waste has led to the destruction of forests and water shortages. We have polluted and contaminated the earth. And it all began with the Industrial Revolution. Our overconsumption of our natural resources of timber, water, coal, iron, copper, silver, and gold to make, take, and waste for just about every product imaginable has led to the crisis the world is now debating.

Industries across the globe tapped into these glorious natural resources to make every kind of goods and services that mankind needed at the time. The more humankind advanced, the more products advanced, depleting the lands and species without giving as much attention to how it was going to manage or use the natural resources. Which leads us to today.

American Awakening

The Industrial Revolution was our great American Awakening. We were growing so much we created an incredibly efficient and productive take-make-dispose machine. Simply, we consumed incredible amounts of raw materials and converted them into final products (as consumers we could use, abuse, and discard), and ultimately dispose of them.

As our human desire to own, possess, and consume things grew, manufacturers produced them at record speeds. We demanded them more and more and companies just kept on producing from food, healthcare products, clothing, you name it, we received it. Whatever we desired and whatever companies could make money at in a cost-effective and efficient way, they delivered.

The railroad industry took off chugging along delivering raw materials to literally every industry imaginable from industrial factories to finished goods and consumers. The more goods produced, the greater the production lines, and the bigger the production processes from across the country that materials began to be sourced from across the globe.

As a world power, global leaders were being pressured to invest in technologies to clean up the mess they had created centuries before. More and more global companies were asked to review their environmental activities and consider a greener approach. Companies were seeing that being environmentally responsible was big business. It just wasn't the right thing to do, it was smart business. Consultants emerged and it was clear; the bigger the enterprise, the greater the pressure arose across the globe to be environmentally aware.

Companies are continually held accountable for any wrong doings. This includes things like illegally disposing of toxins in wells and rivers, transportation leaks, tanker accidents, discharges from factories, drilling blowouts, pollution as a result of poor water treatment facilities, and spills or unchecked gas leaks from oil refineries or pipelines. Or a term bantered about a lot, for hydraulic fracturing (fracking) operations. Fracking is more popular in tapping inaccessible parts of drilled wells or from coalbed wells, tight sand formations, and even shale formations. As new fracking has become so popular, it has been used as much as 90% in new oil wells.

The Santa Rita oil tanker is one the earlier major U.S. oil spills from a tanker in San Francisco Bay in 1907. As a result, public concern became more aware of the damage to water. By World War II public discord about oil leaks reaching U.S. beaches from sinking tankers started to get louder.

In 1967, oil spilled from oil tanker Torrey Canyon, off the coast of England, pouring some 37 million gallons of crude into the water causing considerable environmental damage. It was at that point U.S. President Lyndon B. Johnson put the wheels in motion for greater investigation into oil contamination incidents. As a result, the *Oil Pollution – a Report to the President* was drafted, and the National Oil and Hazardous Substances Pollution Contingency Plan was created. Now this serves as a blueprint for the federal government's National Contingency Plan (NCP) for responding to both oil spills and hazardous waste issues.

Case in point: Look at the evolution from the early days of cheering a geyser of oil spewing in the sky and what was considered successful exploration. By today's standards, that same release would be called a drilling blowout. By all accounts today, the U.S. Environmental Protection Agency would be racing to enlist a national coordination among a hierarchy of responders and contingency efforts to contain the oil release.

Hoping to circumvent any potential issues that might arise from a potential spill in U.S. waters, the federal government set up a remediation plan with specific parameters for addressing spill reporting, containment, and cleanup. As a result, the Clean Water Act (CWA) was created making it illegal to pollute U.S. waters. After a few more iterations and getting a little more enlightened about what the act should cover, the Federal Water Pollution Control Act was put into action. However, by the time 1972 rolled around, the Act was reorganized and expanded to protect the environment and species as well.

Environmental Cause

Fast forward to today, science and technology have given us a front seat into everything that is happening with land, sea, sky, and everything in between. With the help of advanced technology and processes, companies have the ability to locate a site by testing subsoil for onshore exploration or seismic imaging to enable offshore extraction.

Drilling for oil in Alaska, for instance, has only exacerbated the debate about whether Big Oil and others are warming up the climate at unprecedented rates and the potential devastation to Arctic animal habitats that provide biodiversity allowing wildlife to thrive.

And today words like green, circular economy, climate change, and sustainable are all catching the ear of the next generation of corporate leaders. Even Swedish activist Greta Thunberg proved with a little effort anyone can overcome personal challenges and be a changemaker at any age. The 16-year-old achieved global attention as a teenager seeking to strike a climate movement. While her efforts have not completely fallen on deaf ears, they resulted in her receiving a Nobel Peace Prize.

Trying to create moral clarity for climate change is not an easy task by any means. Climate change is about the Earth's climate and weather. As to whether we are in a period of climate change, suggesting we need to alter human activity to achieve better outcomes for the planet, is where the debate begins.

Here's an interesting fact: at the end of 2020, global greenhouse gases were on track to be down more than 6%, as a result of travel bans and the economic slowdown of the COVID-19 pandemic. Many of the global country shutdowns, shelter-in-place orders, and travel-ban restrictions were not expected to be letting up for the foreseeable future, which would also add to the continued emission reductions.

The pandemic awakened our eyes to the realization that GHGs can be reduced in a significant way when we all work together. If the COVID-19 pandemic has taught us anything it's that we can work together to build the type of environment we so desire for future generations. Working together even for a short time we made a difference. With the exception of essential cargo shipments for critical retail products like PPE (personal protective equipment) and other household consumer goods, all travel was halted.

But again, it needs to be acknowledged that the pendulum on the Earth's climate has swung both hot and cold. The early 1980s marked a sharp increase in global temperatures. Many scientists and experts alike drew explicit attention to the year 1988, and particularly the summer, as a pivotal year in propelling global warming into the hot seat for debate.

Much like the Y2K panic, experts sounded the alarm that "global warming" was upon us. The summer of 1988 recorded the hottest at the time, (although we've had hotter since), and we experienced widespread drought in the agricultural regions of the United States and Canada. Couple the droughts with the devastating wildfires in Washington, Oregon, and California in the U.S. and additional fire activity in Europe, Asia, South America, and Africa – global warming seemed very real.

By 1989, a UN environmental official was doing his best impression of Orson Welles's "The War of the Worlds" dramatization when he declared the entire nations extinction would be wiped off the face of the Earth, with rising sea levels as a result of global warming by the year 2000.

Pressure to address global warming was coming from political leaders, and in 1989 the Intergovernmental Panel on Climate Change (IPCC) was established to provide a scientific view of climate and its political and economic impacts.

Countries and governments were being told that they needed to heed the warnings and had a 10-year window of opportunity to solve the GHG effect before it goes beyond human control. Also, in the report they had until 2050, to completely clean up their act or risk wipe-out of all burning coal.

At that time, Vice President Al Gore takes on the cause to raise awareness and end devastation. However, repeatedly debunked by naysayers, global warming didn't resonate with the consuming public. A new mantra of climate change and green emerged. But Gore stuck with the fight and climate change now became part of the educational journey. And it was those two words that were being chanted at rallies and Gore refocused his campaign and the IPCC refocused their efforts, which were awarded the Nobel Peace prize for raising awareness about man-made climate change in 2007 via the documentary *An Inconvenient Truth.*

At this point, global warming has gained a lot of cache' and is in fact, big business. As a business, organization, or individual, if you are not at least paying some attention to the predictions, you must be in denial. The effects of climate change are proving to be apparent as storms, droughts, fires, and floods become stronger and increase with veracity.

Every day our understanding of what needs to be becomes clearer. Not just in the U.S., but across the globe. Corporate leaders from Amazon, BP, Shell, Dell, Trane, Google, and Cargill are feeling the responsibility and even pressure from customers and employees to change their wasteful ways.

Regardless of whether you acknowledge climate change or Green, we can all agree our factories have polluted the air, oil has spilled into our seas, plastics are polluting our oceans, and we are filling our landfills with tons of unnecessary bi-products of our stuff—ultimately all of which is eroding our ecosystems. Mitigation of climate change requires addressing industries like transportation, electricity systems, HVAC, building, agriculture, manufacturing, and more. It requires evaluating migration strategies, long-term planning, resiliency, and opportunities.

The real question, that everyone can agree on, is just how dire is it? Environmentalists are worried the eroding ecosystems will transpire sooner rather than later, while the naysayers want a clear understanding of the parameters. To make change occur, it takes enthusiasts. There's a passage in The Bible (Matthew 4:18), as he was walking by the Sea of

Galilee, he saw two brothers, Simon, who is called Peter and his brother Andrew, casting a net into the sea; they were fishermen. He said to them, "Come after me, and I will make you fishers of men."

The point here is that to be a great leader means reaching everyone—getting people to follow even at the most unusual of times. It does not mean talking to one generation and excluding another. A good educator of climate, green, sustainability, and carbon must have knowledge of the past to move forward. A true influencer understands the mistakes of the past and is able to recognize the opportunities of the future.

It's a true skill. It's about inspiring the masses to be better. In the movie *Field of Dreams*, Kevin Costner's character is struggling with his deceased father, a devoted baseball fan. In the movie, he hears, "If you build it, he will come." The line from the 1989 movie really points out that if he just believes and builds the baseball field, he can make anything happen. Sometimes all it takes is believing and getting others to see the vision.

There are many experiences in our lives that help us to grow and see the world from a different point of view. They give us fresh perspectives. Sometimes just experiencing and seeing with our own eyes can change our view and give us the understanding of how to influence others. We can manifest thoughts' as a reality with the right action. Taking no action, nothing will happen. However, working together increases the probability of improving the environment and the desired outcome.

In today's business climate, it's not uncommon to hear "we must do more with less," as business owners look for ways to run a leaner, cleaner, and more productive operation. Even before recycling was popular, small business owners had a sense of waste management. In the late 1920s, drug stores had a soda fountain and luncheonette inside their retail businesses. The clerk at the time would be known as the "soda jerk."

They were told: 1) Do not over scoop. Sundaes that are made too large are often not eaten and wasted. 2) Be aware of waste when restocking and reaching for items. A stack of fallen napkins means additional cost. Small business owners recognized that simple actions had implications. It's ironic to think almost a century later we are still trying to figure out how to do more with less or even recycle in an incredibly unique and creative way.

Today, more and more attention is being given to sustainability and circularity. It is changing business and an organizational structure. It's changing the way business operates. It's changing the way we think as a society. It's changing history. Whether you believe climate change, circularity, or sustainability is a hoax or not, those who are engaged socially are listening, reacting, and influencing brands.

Case Study
A New Form of Mixologist

Most people don't know that cement production generates roughly 7-8% of the world's industrial CO_2 emissions. But rest assured that's why GCP Applied Technologies is constantly working to find a way to mix it up a tad differently than most. Here's a company that stirs technology and chemistry to create products for the circular economy.

One of the tenets of the circularity is reducing carbon emissions. GCP solutions reduce CO_2 at the point of production and throughout the concrete lifecycle. This starts during the process of creating cement. The process of manufacturing cement is energy intensive, and the chemical reaction in the kiln creates additional carbon dioxide. GCP TAVERO® and OPTEVA® admixtures are used during cement manufacturing and are responsible for reducing CO_2 by about 10 million tons yearly.

During concrete production, admixtures are also used to significantly reduce the volume of cement in the mix while preserving concrete strength. When producers reduce the amount of cement in the mix, they save money and reduce greenhouse gases. GCP's water-reducing concrete admixtures treat 600 million tons of cement, eliminating 100 million tons of CO_2. annually.

A latter step in the lifecycle is what to do with returned concrete. When trucks containing concrete return to the plant, the concrete is typically used to make large blocks or dumped on the ground and allowed to harden. Eventually the large piles of hardened concrete are crushed and hauled away to be landfilled or recycled into base material. Using GCP's CLARENA® RC admixture keeps returned concrete out of landfills, by easily turning each cubic yard of returned concrete into two tons of usable recycled aggregate.

When a truck returns to the production site with returned concrete, the driver simply adds the admixture into the truck drum to produce recycled aggregate. This recycled material can then be sold as high quality, compacted base, or used as a partial replacement for aggregate in fresh concrete. Pretty cool right?

For an industry that is seeking to minimize waste, now it can extract and use fewer natural resources to keep end products out of landfills more, all while generating more revenue.

Food Waste + Innovation

According to the United Nations, the world's population has already soared to a whopping 7.6 billion. It is expected to exceed 9.8 billion by 2050. Just for a moment imagine how dreadful the food waste will become for all those people if this problem is not addressed in a systematic way. Making a shift to circularity affords majors health and environmental benefits when looking at the food chain.

Perhaps this requires taking a step back and discussing why food is wasted? Some food is lost before crops ever leave the farm. Soil is a living environment. Healthy soil is what ensures that crops grow on it and cows graze. Farmers focus on four macro-nutrients to provide healthy soil and crops: nitrogen, phosphorous, potassium, and sulphur.

There are many reasons crops fail. They can vary from farmers overplanting to preparing and controlling for adverse weather, which in some cases can in turn yield a better surplus simply because conditions work in their favor. Even during the early days of the pandemic, some farmers reported destroying their milk and smashing eggs.

Food is also wasted because of retailers setting high-aesthetic standards for fruits and vegetables. Sometimes even the smallest aesthetic imperfection can result in fruits and vegetables being rejected. Simply, the criteria to produce tasty fruits and vegetables, with high nutritional value that is perfectly edible is not an easy task for any farmer. As a result, many fruits and vegetables don't even make it off the trucks.

The good news is that the make-waste industrial economic model is beginning to lose some of its thunder, as new creative startups are beginning to realize they must stop taking from Mother Earth and are leveraging technology to transform business and demand greater corporate responsibility and global leadership.

Fortunately, innovation, maximizing the supply chain, and the desire to be healthier and less wasteful has all led to the creation of companies like Misfits Markets and Hungry Harvest.

Today, Misfits Markets is a subscription box service that offers odd-shaped organically grown fruits and vegetables that are delivered directly to consumers that are much cheaper than traditional grocery store prices. Farmers' report about half of the food grown is discarded simply because of the way it looks. Rather than just wasting food simply because it doesn't look as tasty, Misfits Markets subscription service increases food consumption while greatly impacting the cycle of food waste.

Hungry Harvest, on the other hand, is a farm to doorstep effort. The company has already rescued 20 million pounds of food waste. Evan Lutz's story was so compelling Shark Tank's very own Robert Herjavec made a deal to acquire a 10% stake in Hungry Harvest to help it reduce food waste and provide food relief to insecure communities around the world.

The farm-to-table supply chain is improving, but when it is lost or broken, fruits, vegetables, dairy, and meat are extremely vulnerable, and in low-income countries, harvesting damaged produce or poor yield can mean everything.

Here's what we know about food waste or food loss. While they may be commonly used terms, they do not mean the same thing, according to the Food and Agriculture Organization (FAO).

- Food loss: means food that is in the early stages of production harvest, storage, and transportation. Much of this is a result of storage facilities, poor handling, packaging, and transportation.

- Food waste: means items that are edible and/or for human consumption but are tossed away by consumers or supermarkets or farmers.

Sometimes all it takes is data to be the sweetest ingredient. The IBM Food Trust is just one example of how blockchain technology is impacting the complex food supply chain. Food safety has many players involved in getting food from the grower to the final consumer. As a result, it's hard to keep track of what's happening along the way to a particular product. Food traceability is really something we react to especially when we are talking about putting a product like food in our body. It's more than just feeding our children and getting the data. It's about having that end-to-end visibility that is so absolutely critical in making us all feel comfortable about what our family is consuming.

Food Trust leverages blockchain digitized data in a way that creates visibility, and it opens the door to increased supply-chain efficiencies and less food waste. As consumer preferences continue to change and they want to save on pricing, increased safety, and bettering the environment, this will continue to become more important to those who care about food loss and eliminating food waste. This gives everyone a window into where products are coming from, who made them, what happened to them on route, and how long they've been on the shelf.

So now that we have tracked the food from the store to our home, how do consumers eliminate the amount of food they waste, adding to the excessive amount?

The right food supply-chain tracking and tracing tool can eliminate food waste and food loss. There are even apps to prevent food that is unusable or inedible from being turned to garbage. One company, U.K.-based OLIO has created an app that is all about taking a picture of your item(s) and sharing it with your friends, neighbors, or whoever you want. What makes this app work so well is food that is ending its sell-by date is not tossed away like yesterday's news, rather, the surplus food is shared. In the United States, cans of food have been shared with soup kitchens or food pantries for years.

Consider the OLIO app for a moment. Simply with a photo, local stores can share home-grown vegetables, bread from a baker, or the groceries in your fridge, nearing their end date can be entered in an OLIO app, no longer being thrown away, and end up on someone else's menu.

Other apps help individuals keep from throwing away the food that is truly inedible. When you do need to dispose of food or scrap, make sure to compost. Composting diverts waste from landfills and reduces methane emissions. Some households are diverting as much as 150 KG (330-lbs.) annually, according to the FAO.

Another company connects the dots with a global waste-management system using a digital map to connect individuals and their food scraps with those who are composting. Based in Sydney, Australia, ShareWaste helps individuals who want to either collect food scraps or contribute them to a nearby neighborhood compost system.

Here's an idea: recycling coffee grounds into coffee cups? Kaffeeform, from creator Julian Lechner, has discovered a way to recycle coffee grounds. After three years of putting his ingenuity to use, he has transformed renewable raw materials into a durable robust material, which he calls Kaffee cup. A guy on a bike collects used coffee grounds from select cafes in Berlin, Germany, and delivers them to plants to be compounded and shaped into coffee cups and then they get the final polishing to create a new product.

What have we learned so far? Applying the circular economy to food is all about designing out waste and cleaner air, keeping products and materials in use, and restoring the natural ecosystems. It's interesting to examine regenerating food cycles. Think about how it all began. In the Old Testament (Genesis 1: 28-30) God's message, "Be fertile and multiply: fill the earth and subdue it. Have dominion over the fish of the sea, the birds in the air, and all the living things that move on the earth." God also said: "See I give you every seed-bearing plant all over the earth and every tree that has seed-bearing fruit on it be your food; and to all the animals of the land, all the birds of the air, and all the living creatures that crawl on the ground. I give all the green plants for food..."

Up to this point we have learned for billions of years; the earth has been able to thrive and sustain. But the pace at which humankind is taking from the earth, it can't thrive, and the ecosystem is struggling. And, in fact, in some regions, it is unable to continue to produce food for the next cycle of life, as was originally intended. So, the question remains, is humankind destroying the food's natural ecosystem from which it began?

Repurposing Goods

It's particularly important to understand that the idea of repurposing, reusing, and recycling pieces is as old as mankind itself. Consider this example. The History Channel's TV Series *Forged in Fire* demonstrates the idea of recycling, reusing, and repurposing very well. On this show, world-class bladesmith recreate historical edged weapons.

They demonstrate how they can melt and produce an axe of similar quality that is on display. Interestingly, the point here, is that not every piece can be easily reused. And not every part of an axe can be replicated exactly the same way. However, if your bronze axe broke, you could, just like the bladesmith, re-create an axe by melting it and producing an axe of similar quality to serve the same purpose. For years, we have called that process recycling.

Dell, for instance, uses closed-loop plastics to make new parts for computers and monitors, as its pledge to the environment. Each year it recycles millions of pounds of closed-loop plastics to produce new parts for new computers and monitors. The Red Rock, Texas-based company explains that after older computers and monitors, etc., are disassembled, the plastics are shredded, and melded with other virgin plastics. Dell reports the average closed-loop recycled content of the resins amounts to 30-35%.

Dell is not alone. When it comes to leveraging closed-loop plastic recycling, HP has been taking that to heart for decades. Since launching a recycling program in 1991, HP numbers show it has kept 875 million cartridges, 114 million apparel hangers, and 4.69 billion postconsumer plastic bottles out of landfills, upcycling them to make new HP products. That means, since 2018, HP has reduced as much as 5% of its plastic packaging, as a result.

Even Cisco has jumped on the bandwagon, making a 100% commitment to product returns by providing product return pickup and transport at no cost. It is also working to create services that extend the useful life of products currently in use, and repurposing returned products and components in new product manufacturing.

But does it all work? Are we saving our planet from total extinction? While the world continues to debate the issue, there is much more that can be done to ease the damage on the environment. While recycling has proven to be a good idea in its own right, it has proven to be fraught with challenges, thus opening the door to fresh aggressive innovators. This is how the take-make-waste vision started to find its way into the hearts and minds of a younger and even more progressive generation.

Today the younger generation is looking to make a fashion statement with refurbished clothing. Makes you wonder if a show like HBO's series *Sex in the City* would have helped the planet since they had an unquestionable thirst to purchase the latest in fashion accessories. (Can you say Manolo Blahnik)?

With the recent pandemic, many fashion designers have finally caught on and are designing with the environment in mind. It's interesting to note that of the 213 targets set following the Copenhagen Fashion Summit in 2017, it seems under 30% have been hit. Part of the challenge is that companies are struggling to increase the amount of recycled material used for clothing.

Who would have ever thought that clothing that can be kept in service, refurbished, and worn again and again would be better for the planet? Well, it's happening with some of the biggest denim brand names in the business and even creative startups.

Canadian retailer Frank and Oak, for instance, says it uses denim from post-consumer waste. These are those worn-out jeans that were headed to landfills and are instead collected and redirected to a fabric recycler where they are shredded, broken down, and then re-spun into new materials. The company itself has a circularity plan: by 2022, it plans to cut all virgin plastic out of its supply chain by using only recycled polyester bags, removing excess shipment packaging, and maximizing raw materials.

The fashion runways have always been a way to display bright new interesting colors to the world each year. However, as more and more environmentally conscious buyers make their way to fashion shows, it will be interesting to see what Vogue and others reveal as hot new looks in an attempt to avoid filling landfills.

Many clothing companies are jumping on the circular bandwagon to recycle jeans and so much more. Think of it this way, the clothing that no one wants is deemed as "wiped clothing" or refurbished or shredded for things like insulation in mattress stuffing; or fibers from old sweaters are recaptured and they are reused for new garments. Clothing that is reused, or otherwise kept in service and worn again, is better for the planet as the material and energy that went into making them is not replaced, or is it?

Cradle to Cradle

For decades, we have heard environmentalists preach that as a society we need to repurpose, reuse, or upcycle as a means to stop destroying the environment. They insisted almost religiously that humankind was destroying the environment, taking all of its natural resources and not giving anything back. They have dissected this subject stressing unless we alter our ways that we will deplete our most precious resources. This cry for Mother Nature has been going on for decades.

So, what makes this declaration today any different than previous ones? Why should you be paying attention now? Some believe the circular economy movement is different from its predecessor for many reasons. Perhaps, as the saying goes, with age comes experience.

And unlike this preaching approach, this movement has taken a few cues and learned from the past, creating strategies that bridge previous views with a new vision of reduce, reuse, and recycle. In addition, this new concept helps people recognize you don't have to own everything, and that goods and services can be reused for better purposes.

Pretty impressive! That's why authors, William McDonough, visionary architect by trade, and Michael Braungart, a chemist, collaborated as experts in their fields to develop cradle-to-cradle concepts and put them into practice.

It's really a pretty simple approach once you get the hang of the Four R's: reduce, reuse, recycle, and regulate. Some even refer to it as cutting back and simplifying. McDonough and Braungart, authored *Cradle to Cradle, 2002,* noting in their book, waste can be recreated to produce something even better and less expensive than buying new material. We are seeing many industries being formed using food waste, metals, and even coffee beans. Anything can be reimagined and reused, even if only part of the way, if you can imagine it.

Taking these ideas, a step further, now we are not just renting or owning all the products and things, but we are sharing them over and over again. Can you say Airbnb, Uber, or Bosch? We've pondered this age-old question: should we rent or buy? The rent vs. buy question has provided greater value for different reasons. For many decades, we debated this question about our homes and more recently even our cars. And today, this option extends to every device, tool, and piece of equipment that comes to mind. Thus, today's ridesharing and home rentals have become big business and people are doing it more and more for ecological reasons. These companies have successfully transformed a product-oriented approach into a service platform.

How about ridesharing and car-sharing platforms that have opened up their services to not only taking people place-to-place, but they also offer services to instantly deliver food, electronics, cosmetics, and just about anything else you need. This is even happening in urban areas, cities can offer bike sharing and electric scooter services as a low-carbon alternative, rather than ownership, and integrate this into public transportation. This means consumers no longer need to own everything and they can share more goods and services. Innovators, basically, if you've got an idea or product, consumers will consume it in one form or another.

Now seems the perfect time to embrace the circular journey to recycle bottles, cans, paper, and plastics in many communities. It might have taken many years, but many cities, towns, communities, states, and countries have finally gotten on board with the concept of repurposing, recycling, and finally reusing products for the good of the planet.

Yale University, for instance, has a circularity goal to improve and advance its purchasing standards that promote sustainability and resilience. As part of that initiative the university is working toward creating, piloting, and assessing a "pay as you throw" system to be implemented by January 2022. It is also working on implementing a waste reduction goal to identify the most impactful commodity groups that contribute to Yale's waste stream, through material flow analyses.

Making a pledge to go circular is a start. Going circular is more than just saying the words. It means changing employees' attitudes. It requires participatory approaches to change hearts and minds within an organization or country. Countries need to have a roadmap. Countries need to have a clear strategy established for achieving goals by a set date. The more things change it becomes time to walk the talk.

It's the who, what, how, when, where, and why of going circular that needs to be addressed. To date, we have seen countries like Finland and France make a strong commitment to a circular effort.

The European Community supports the value of a circular economy. In fact, it adopted the principles of the package in 2014 in an effort to encourage member states to establish a clear roadmap for success. Since that time only a few states have been able to move forward. Many have talked about wanting to go circular, but each are at different stages of the process.

The Netherlands has pledged to go fully circular by 2050, and still has much work to reach it goals. It started the journey even before the EU showed support for any kind of resource management programs.

London has a circular plan, which originally had a route map ending in 2036. It has since been adjusted with the end point for the London Plan now slated for 2041. Finland jumped on board in 2016 and has a roadmap for 2026 that has been updated to 2030 to include striving to cut its carbon footprint in half from the level of 2010. France and Slovenia have also published strategies and Italy is working on one. Germany has indicated it is engaged in the circularity process.

Whatever each country does most likely will not be consistent in the United States. Each country follows their own public procurement rules about what is considered a circular product and services. Coordination by countries will create greater opportunities of course, but as we can all agree, there will also be many missed opportunities.

Case Study
Don't Get Lost in the Jargon
Companies are doing sustainability. Sustainability needs to be part of the day-to-day work. As a company, understanding what sustainability means by first defining it, and working with communities on a shared vision is essential. Some of the best advice perhaps is don't think of it as circular economy, but rather as part of the everyday culture.

To a company like Bechtel, achieving sustainability begins with design, material sourcing, continuing through construction to work toward the least amount of waste and water consumption for the community.

According to Bechtel's Global Head of Sustainability Tam Nguyen, it's a shared vision with the community and stakeholders. It's about creating and enabling the environment the team is working in and benefiting the community in the long term.

Bechtel has been working diligently to integrate the United Nations sustainable goals across everything it does by 2030.

One example, Bechtel likes to point to is the work it was part of in the Bechtel-Enka Joint Venture, in South Caucasus Pipeline Expansion (SCPx) Project in the Republic of Georgia. The project includes building two compressor stations, a metering and pressure-reducing station, and associated access roadways at several locations across the country along an existing pipeline.

Nguyen described this as a little city because at the peak period of work there were some 4,175 workers spread across three sites and another 1,945 people living on camps set up for the project. In order to mitigate the impact on the community Bechtel and the customer had to be innovative. As part of this development these little communities had to function like traditional towns, providing their own energy, waste system, and sourcing.

Even all the water was being reused, retreated, and repurposed. Excess water was provided to the community. Food waste was even separated and sent to a food dryer system that removed water content. The dried food waste was then sent to biomass units to be burned. The heat generated was used in boilers that provided hot water to camp residents. Nguyen explained, it wasn't perfect, but it was happening and that it was circular.

The Bechtel project and environmental engineer re-looked at the data. They were collecting data like how much waste they were not transporting to a landfill and connecting the dots to really show how this was all reducing carbon, waste, and water.

It is at this point that Bechtel began to more closely realize how the circular economy and social sustainability bring benefits to communities, and ultimately, to the bottom line. The numbers speak for themselves. Bechtel estimated a potential savings of nearly $1 million a year in costs.

Bechtel reports it saved about 371,316 gallons per year of fuel, cut water usage down to 100,000 gallons (378,541 liters) per year, reduced 90% (990 kg/workday) of food waste; and recovered, reused, and recycled 40% of construction waste annually.

Data through circularity is the real story. Over the long run it was apparent Bechtel was able to develop a deeper understanding of the savings on the project. Ultimately, by garnering a better idea of the addressable savings for Bechtel means remaining savings opportunities for other stakeholders in the process.

Linear to Innovative Design

The world is now at a crossroads. More companies and individuals need to move away from damaged linear thinking and build on the role of design and innovative products that leverage the thoughtful consumption of natural resources that lead to better outcomes for the world.

We will begin to witness a shift from the make-take-waste way of thinking with manufacturers, to a transformative shift in designing and building the best products right from conception. Leveraging design processes, we can expect the use of the digital twin and Internet of Things (IoT) to create expansive digital models of the environment and all its products. Through highly secure digital replicas we can now create even more solutions that drive the customer experience in ways to help our future generations see a much cleaner and brighter ecosystem.

With the IoT, manufacturers are selling services, rather than just products. It's now in everything we do. We've already discussed the Amazon effect. Now we are talking software-as-a-service. Innovative methods of design thinking are essential as the world's population is massively growing and we need to align all these efforts with sustainable goals to reduce and eliminate the unnecessary consumption of natural resources.

Signify is one company. The Philips Lighting brand designs streets lights and components with recycled parts. In fact, the company has a circular strategy program to double revenue by 32% by 2025. Interactive software manages, monitors, and controls lighting systems, luminaires, sensors, and connected devices from Signify and other manufacturers. Philips also encourages other businesses to take advantage of its LED connected lighting with embedded IoT sensors and software to manage and optimize building efficiency to create a sustainable smart office.

Unlike the natural ecosystem, which operate in cycles — plants grow in soil, animals eat plants, dung replenishes soils — the industrial economy is largely linear, with generally four types of raw materials-minerals, ores, fossil fuels, and biomass.

Designing Foods

Consider for a moment our food habits and preferences. The foods we eat must be healthy and nutritional, but we also have to think about the way it is being designed. When designing new products, the first place to start with is, of course, the first meal of the day, through all our snacks, to the end of the day, dinner or supper depending on what part of the world you are from.

That means considering choices including cereals to all the other meals that are consumed throughout the day. It's interesting to recognize that for decades our food choices really have not been our own. They have been designed by our society—by employers, retailers, restaurants, schools, hospitals, restaurants, and other providers.

So, here's the point, in a regenerative environment, we all need to reconsider what we make and consume. That means reconsidering our food choices every day. Moving forward, food manufacturers and other companies will need to reshape our food preferences and habits once again. Cities need to create new menus based on a fundamentally different food system.

Bear in mind that in a circular economy the concept here is food products are designed to be healthy and nutritional, but most importantly, we can't forget how they are made. Depending on the type, taste, and smell food specialties can look at microorganisms such as (Algae, Bacteria Yeast, Fungi) or plants (Pulses, Grains) or cell cultures or even, insect-based (can you say cricket cookies?).

This means designers of food products and recipes that reuse ingredients can be safely returned into the soil or water supply. Simply, we are designing out waste and improving healthier choices.

In this way food designers can play their part in designing out food waste. Marketing can position these delicious and healthy products as easy and accessible choices for people on a daily basis.

Case Study
Field of Food Dreams
Perhaps it's the development of a healthier, wiser, and more ecologically sustainable crop that that has inspired the Dominican Sisters of Adrian, Michigan to believe, if you build it, it will grow. The campus is facilitating regenerative approaches and the incorporation of permaculture as it produces food for the residents throughout the year all while bringing about positive agricultural change to the environment.

The total land is about 108 acres, of which, about 30 acres have buildings on them, and around these building is normative. In 2012 they began farming seven acres on the southeast corner of the property. Now for the past eight years, the sisters have built up the kitchen gardens by adding raising bed gardening. The Sisters garden in the raised beds as a means to keep them engaged with the Earth even as they move into their older years.

Originally part of this land was dedicated as tennis courts. However, these courts were no longer used with the closing of the school. The Sisters decided to remove the asphalt courts and apply the permaculture principles to crop the land.

The farm has grown fruit, vegetables, and flowers, as well as protects natural species like monarch butterflies with milkweed. The farm is almost entirely self-sustained on the fruits and vegetables it grows as it uses the natural rainfall for watering.

By making low-cost improvements to the land, the Dominican sisters can increase their overall household food security and increase a regenerative process of the land. The ultimate goal is to continue to grow food for the campus and strive for being, at least partially, self-sufficient in their food dependency while building soil health.

The Adrian Dominican Sisters, a congregation of some 500 vowed religion women and 211 Associates, minister in 22 states and four countries: the Dominican Republic, the Philippines, Mexico, and Norway, recognize that locally grown food needs to be a grassroots movement in sustainable farming. Raising awareness about the benefits of how permaculture and how implementation of their sustainable farming efforts is a way to share knowledge and their hands-on experience about the process with others.

Director of Sustainability, Corinne Sanders, explained the Dominican sisters are passionate about local food, locally grown food, and food that's grown through regenerative agriculture that gives back into the land what has been taken. Spreading their teachings is where the sisters do a lot of education with their university students at Siena Heights University, Adrian, Michigan, which is located next door to their main residence and Barry University in Miami Shores, Florida.

The goal for the sisters is to expand on what they have been learning and sharing with students. Sanders acknowledges it's about more resilient living outside of what's just here at their campus and what the sisters are currently doing.

She noted the bigger goal is to make these regenerative communities bigger and to share with multi-generational families so they can achieve the same success and to build on this foundation and even do more. Ultimately, they are continuing to teach permaculture, food security, and community recovery.

Just like the Dominican sisters described in this example, food creators will need to consider all sorts of creative options for meat and dairy. The underpinnings of permaculture draw on the thinking of ethical design of taking care of the earth and the fair share of the surplus.

"There is one, and only one solution, and we almost have no time to try it. We must turn all our resources to repairing the natural world and train all our young people to help. They want to; we need to give them this last chance to create forests, soils, clean waters, clean energies, secure communities, stable regions, and to know how to do it from hands-on experience."

Bill Mollison,
Australian scientist

Permaculture Design

The feasibility and benefits of local sourcing has been the subject of intense scrutiny and debate for many years. While urban farming can provide cities with certain vegetables and even fruits, the bigger challenge is rising populations.

All of the urban developments are negatively impacting the one billion people living in informal settlements and slums worldwide. And pandemics like COVID-19 are also having a greater impact on the poor and densely populated areas.

Permaculture is a design science based on the principles of ecological design and sustainability of the natural ecosystems. This is all rooted in the observation of positive results from the creation and managing of systems for food, medicine, water, and more.

The permaculture lessons are based on the ethics — earth care, people care, and fair share — that guide the use of the 12 design principles. These principles, when applied correctly, are seen as universal and they offer a roadmap for cultural and biological growth. The underpinnings are rooted in the overall soil architecture, Earth's shaping, 3D vegetation growing, optimization of resources (water, nutrients), creation of natural balance, and usage of animals and indigenous native plants embedded in closed loops.

While the teachings of how we live on the land first came from the indigenous cultures, it wasn't until Bill Mollison (professor) and David Holmgren (student at this time) at the University of Tasmania, Australia, coined this popular term in the late-1970s. The permaculture design system was taught as actual principles of an applied design system in 1981.

It is projected that some 60% of the world's population will live in cities by 2030. As a result, rapid urbanization will account for 70% of the global carbon emissions and more than 60% of resources used. The issue here is the inadequate infrastructure and services — things like waste collection and water and sanitary systems, roads and bridges, air pollution and unplanned urban sprawl — is rapidly increasing.

As all of these developments contribute to the overall changes in people's dietary expectations and nutritional needs, it's almost impossible for traditional farmers to accommodate the broader demands of billions of people in cities today. This has led to more cities and communities looking to source greater amounts of food.

Take, for example, regenerative approaches to food production. This is a system that improves the health and local food that enters cities to be cultivated in a way that enhances rather than degrades the natural environment. This includes making other systemic benefits.

Regenerative practices support the development of healthy soils, which can result in foods with improved taste and micronutrient content. Let the numbers speak for themselves. The Food and Agriculture Organization says there are only 60 global harvests left, and within this generation we may have as many as 9 billion people to feed.

Communities need support to implement techniques. Every company, individual, and community has an opportunity to step up and reverse anything that destroys the natural environment.

As technology continues to advance, we need young farmers and cities to collaborate to build soil fertility to prevent any further soil destruction and develop specific systems to achieve greater community benefits. Some of these new practices include shifting from synthetic to organic fertilizers, employing crop rotation, and using greater crop variation to promote biodiversity. There is also farming types such as agroecology, rotational grazing, agroforestry, conservation agriculture, and permaculture.

Broadly speaking, being regenerative incorporates many of the farming methods for permaculture to restore and environmentally enhance the natural environment.

In addition, we are seeing more technology advances in areas of aquaculture, which is the breeding and harvesting of fish, algae, shellfish, and other organisms in any and all water environments. Also, there's been some amazing advances in hydroponics, a method of growing plants, in a controlled, soilless setting.

As we look back at history during the past several decades, it's no wonder there are some clear underlying truths about how we have arrived at our current linear take-make-waste mess we find ourselves in today. Many of the hurdles stem from our insatiable buying habits that only seemed to blossom, the more we as a society were offered and the more as consumers, we were willing to purchase from electronics to food to just about anything life had to offer. While history often repeats itself, and we hope not a prophecy as some have already stated, we all need to examine our past with a closer eye to make the necessary changes for future generations.

We can all sit back and postulate about how to solve the environmental crises, but the world needs individuals and companies that will lead by example. It needs the doers and the innovators that will accelerate change for future generations to step up!

CHAPTER 4

SUSTAINABILITY

Sustainability 101

Merriam-Webster defines sustainable as relating to or being a method of harvesting or using a resource so that the resource is not depleted or permanently damaged. Simply put, it is environmentally sound living without compromising the needs of future generations.

Today many refer to sustainability as corporate, social, responsibility (CSR) or environmental, social, and governance (ESG). If you peel back the layers of the onion, you will discover the sustainability conversation is somewhat more complex depending on how you view it and your interpretation of it. In fact, all too often people will inadvertently use the acronyms CSR and ESG and the word sustainability interchangeably.

Acronyms are funny things. They can mean a lot of things, but that doesn't mean they may be correct for everything. Naturally, in the aforementioned case they can be the right definition, but they shouldn't be used in the same sentence.

Look at it this way, when talking about CSR we are talking about the best practices to uphold corporate governance that comes from disclosing and even benchmarking data and information. These are the ways you measure your sustainable development goals. There is a distinct set of objectives and governance guidelines. A key difference when interpreting the role and function of each objective and how to be economically sustainable to the environment.

It's profoundly essential to grasp the role corporate social responsibility plays in the bigger picture of sustainability. It's really about leaving something for the next generations. Drilling down even further, on the most basic level, it's all about being more sustainable through development practices, as it relates to being outstanding eco-friendly citizens in a global society.

These precepts serve to provide greater transparency in disclosure reporting for stakeholders, consumers, and partners. It's all about a sustainable stewardship for our economy, environment, and society.

Governance

While the bigger discussion always starts with sustainability, it requires reporting and demonstrating greater detail of each pillar, and that means drilling down (environmental, social, and governance) to scope, practice, strategy, and execution for capital-project opportunities, and this then becomes more complex and requires a substantial shift in the way companies measure and disclose performance.

Now when we talk about how we would define sustainability, typically it is painted with a broad brush using a much larger canvass. It's all about improving the environment or being green. You know, doing well by doing good. And that is why we often see the words corporate responsibility associated with sustainability.

Think of environmental, social, governance (ESG) for the capital markets. More specifically when reviewing and even identifying superior risk-adjusted returns. Most recently, ESG has picked up some recognition among other industries, including commercial real estate.

This shift in nomenclature has felt sudden to some. However, the emphasis placed on all three of these ESG pillars along with the time involved in planning and implementing necessary changes tells us it's time for companies to collect, report, and act on ESG data.

When examining the broader sustainability issue, it's important to look beyond just climate. In the current context, a lot of attention is increasingly being brought on non-financial, environmental, social, and governance factors.

Not just for sustainability issues, but when examining the competitiveness issues to win marketshare and investment across the ESG investing, some put the dollars at about $30 trillion in investment worldwide. It's important to recognize, there is a lack of market integrity and transparency in some of these assets. That is why it is essential to have a better definition, and understanding of the criteria, and the impact assessments outlined. A problem still exists that companies can receive high-credit rating for the E metrics (or the environmental part of ESG metrics) but still be a remarkably, high carbon-intensive corporation.

Perhaps another point to consider is the concept ESG is used in relation to investing and philanthropy. Oftentimes it is used to evaluate financial performance for measuring positive outcomes such as decreasing costs, improving profitability, and better energy efficiency. Ultimately, these companies will provide better behavior to evaluate the future financial performance by measuring their sustainability. U.S. and European-based companies alike recognize the money flowing into ESG. Impact investing and philanthropy have increased significantly in recent years and as a result we are seeing more companies view corporate social responsibility (CSR) as part of environmental strategies.

When we look at what other countries are doing, they tend to look at CSR as being more socially accountable to make a positive environmental impact. There is clearly no one way to achieve corporate sustainability. It's all about being a socially conscious environment, coupled with employees, partners, and customers.

Organizations need to really think of CSR as part of the global core strategy, business operations, and reporting metrics. It needs to be positive, with a stronger focus on social, as well as environmental, disclosure, and programs. While the term corporate social responsibility is widely used in the business community and among families, the word sustainability has been an eye opener for a myriad of businesses.

Better Tomorrow

Corporate sustainability is on the rise within companies and it is driving significant cultural change within organizations and individuals. Let's just say it's creating a global gold rush. We are witnessing it in terms of how actions and behaviors are creating corporate transformation and its social and environmental impact.

This metamorphosis is pushing companies and individuals to make a significant transformation from now until 2030. But then continue to work even harder to achieve Scope 3 emissions before 2050.

Emissions are separated in Scopes 1, 2, and 3.

Scope 1:   Direct emissions created from your sources or activities. These are your own heating, cooling, fleets, machines, vehicles.

Scope 2:   Indirect emission that is sourced from energy providers that power your office or home (simply the electricity that you purchase).

Scope 3:   Transferred indirect emissions. This means everything you are engaged in from disposal of trash, purchased goods which encompasses the entire supply chain including business travel of your team, electricity of the entire product lifecycle all your customers consume.

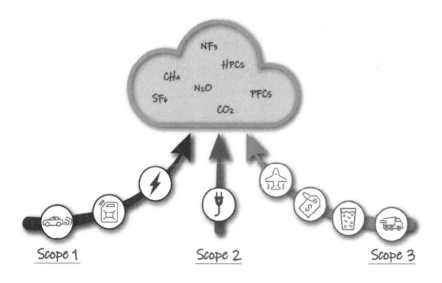

For years, companies have talked about taking care of the Mother Earth. But the mission now needs to focus on more than just the concept of the planet, but its ecosystem, and the people, which in turn will ensure profitable returns for all. This is the cycle for a successful global environment.

In fact, it's no wonder that generative family businesses like Mars Corporation, makers of M&M, Petcare, and more, have a deep understanding that the long-term future of its business depends on its commitment to the planet. It is constantly trying to reimagine the way business is conducted.

This is a company that asks the tough question: how can an almost 110-year-old company sustain itself for another century? What is the long-term view with a focus on stewardship across generations that encompasses profit, people, technology, and the planet?

With no interest or desire in selling in the immediate future or even entertaining such an idea to the highest bidder, this is a company that is making Mars sustainable today. What CSR-type of questions needs to be considered in today's ever-changing world? Today's real success story is driven by understanding the planet first. Any conversation you have with Mars associates illustrates what the guiding philosophy is and what a differentiator is in a highly competitive marketplace. It's obvious this differentiator has helped the Mars machine grow, acquire, and stay a steady course, which ultimately has led to its success.

Back in 2017, Mars conversations led leaders to take the posture that profit, while critical, of course; it needed to focus on sustained profitability. That meant it needed to be steadfast about its people, the planet, and long-term sustainability.

Over the years much work has been done; and even more can be imagined, actually.

For a company that is betting billions of dollars on the right choices, a philosophical commitment is paramount. But a tenacious commitment to community, planet, and understanding the significance of real business metrics is what matters most. The dogged business heads at Mars need to see that numbers work. More importantly, they are seeing that sustainability is answering the difficult questions for a better tomorrow.

ESG Endowments

These new circular business models and improved resource efficiencies should open more opportunities for a restorative and regenerative economy that potentially could generate as much as $4.5 trillion by 2030.

A key point Peter Adriaens, professor of finance and entrepreneurship in Civil and Environmental Engineering at the University of Michigan made is that consumers will increasingly buy products based on knowledge of how sustainable the product is or isn't. And that means you can expect pressure on pension fund investment allocations in funds that include for plastics, for instance, that are non-sustainable or do not serve the common good.

Some investment fund allocation to unsustainable holdings have been frozen, amid the COVID pandemic, supply-chain environmental concerns, and political transitions – which is not uncommon during political elections and other societal shifts. How long those types of changes linger is really anyone's guess.

Ultimately, these types of holdings, alongside the endowment asset managers are going to respond accordingly. Universities, for instance, often are challenged to influence certain decisions. Take for example the University of Michigan, which has some 340 investment managers across all financial asset classes. These investment managers are not at the university, but rather they are third parties that the university relies on to essentially invest the endowment capital.

One of the biggest decisions university endowments are struggling with is the decision of whether to divest from energy. Consider Adriaens point that energy divestment is tricky because, until fairly recently it was an incredibly attractive value proposition for investors, with high returns and high dividends, which every investor likes. It's no surprise then, energy companies and projects almost always were part of the portfolio of pretty much every pension fund, endowment, and every sovereign wealth fund.

Now, students and others are creating a whole movement to ask the endowment to divest from fossil fuel energy. What the endowment managers have to consider is where to take all this money out of fossil energy projects and where will they put it, in order to secure similar returns that they were getting from the energy holdings—and this is creating a sea-change of disruption. But that's not the only consideration.

There is a second consideration that the university endowments reflect the values of the university community which include political, environmental, and social dimensions. Many of the donors to endowments are wealthy individuals (alums) who have an investment strategy that may not mirror that of the university.

If alumni achieve better returns by remaining in fossil fuels, they may decide not to continue to give to - or defer giving to—endowments. Consideration for what might be better for the social or societal good versus what is best for the operations of the university become entangled. Candidly, if the endowment returns go down, that results in less money to be spun off and actually put into university operations. Even post-COVID, revenues will likely continue to decrease for universities as student registration may decline.

Looking at endowments through another lens, universities will need to keep an eye on the performance of fixed and some variable costs as a result of declining tuition fees and additional returns that the endowment will be required to generate. It's really a money mass balance. And mass balance of societal benefits.

It comes down to transitioning traditional energy supplies through solar supplies and energy efficiency, recycling programs, water bottle refilling stations, organic farming, reimbursements for going green, shuttle buses and carpooling, and so much more on campuses.

The University of Michigan is just like any other university, and of course, is part of the Big Ten, which means it has a lot of operational expenditures and capital investments. For instance, campus buses are run on biodiesel or electricity. It is transitioning its HVAC systems to use renewables and is investing in solar parks on its campuses. It is also looking at transitioning to natural gas.

The energy discussion has to be viewed via two separate lenses. One is the operational lens of a university, which aims to transition to net zero carbon. There is an extremely high priority that renewable energy becomes a big part of the discussion, a big part of the deployment. The second is the endowment where it's really more about the university investing its capital from which it draws funds to support operations. This includes investment in fellowships as well as investments in the campus all while improving buildings and whatever else it does to ensure resilience and adaptation to this ever-changing climate change.

Plastics as Destruction

Plastics, of course, are one of the scourges of the ocean and of an industrial society. In many ways, it's driven by consumerism, by all the products companies manufacture and sell to meet consumer demand. The trends of plastics in society has been increasing since the 1960s.

From a cultural perspective there are many movements taking place in society as a result of consumer expectations. And actually, a lot of that is also being driven by the companies themselves as products are being made cheaper with plastics components. But it's more than the products that end up in the ocean, it's also all the packaging as part of the supply chain.

Consumers are becoming a lot more environmentally aware. The companies, governments, and financial institutions recognize the harm plastics inflicts on the environment. The purchasing power of the buying public is becoming much more discerning. And the influence of all these organizations is having a positive impact on overall business models. Simply, sustainably minded consumers are putting their money where they believe it is doing the least amount of damage. Ultimately, we are voting with our wallets.

By reconsidering investment practices and models what emerges is new sustainability-driven strategies and activities in the business community and ESG metrics-rated investments in pension funds. Companies can begin to look at innovation alternatives for single-use plastics. These new and emerging solutions go well beyond recycled or re-used products.

In 2017, a plastics consortium was formed in an effort to streamline plastics heading into the ocean. Today member companies Dell, Bureo, Herman Millar, IKEA, HP, General Motors, Humanscale, Interface, Trek Bicycles and Solgaard all participate in the NextWave Plastics coalition. Many support the plastics consortium in an effort to divert 25,000 metric tons of plastics (1.2 billion single-use plastic water bottle) from entering the ocean by end of 2025.

They are working to achieve this mission by following 10 principles that range from transparency to open-source, accountable, science-based, beneficial, enduring, and complementary, to create a lasting reduction to zero plastic flowing into waterway and the oceans. NextWave likes to say it is convened by Lonely Whale and supported by a host of global thought leaders in scientific research environmental advocacy that make it all possible.

As a society we have littered oceans at the cost of destroying Mother Earth. It's not just the fossil fuels from our cars or to heat our homes, it's the junk we throw away every day. We watch as our rivers, waterways, and oceans suffer, as we mindlessly let waste flow in them. Waste collects in places we will never be able to retrieve, destroying natural species as rotten smells pollute the air. Our beautiful waterways have become modern day trash bins. And plastics, when exposed for a long time to seawater, degrade to smaller particles which are difficult to remove and detrimentally impact sea life.

The consortia work with third parties that capture plastic as it goes from rivers, or manufacturing plants, or waste facilities to the ocean. Adriaens makes a strong point, saying computers are still comprised of large chunks of product that if handled properly, can be captured, and recycled for reintegrated material, for example, into our electronics equipment.

Dell computer manufacturers about 40% recycled plastic. HP says it plans to increase recycled content in its products to 30% by 2025. It also intends to eliminate 75% of single-use plastic from its packaging by 2024.

And a lot of that recycled plastic tends to wash from rivers to oceans. HP is trying to make a difference. Its HP Elite Dragonfly notebook uses just a small amount of the ocean-bound plastic, recycled from litter collected in Haiti. HP sources millions of plastic bottles, and in fact, the company reports 82% of all the mechanical parts on its HP Elite Dragonfly notebooks are made of recycle materials. And the outer packaging is 100% sustainably sourced.

Just think about the products, for instance, a company like Best Buy sells in the United States. The big-box retailer is known for selling electronics, the packaging alone from the products it sells is considerable. The good news is Best Buy has set sustainability goals to reduce carbon emissions to address climate change and to be carbon neutral by 2040.

Fourth Pillar

Many organizations insist the three pillars are the most important when we talk about sustainability. These pillars include the environmental, social, and governance metrics. The fourth pillar is digital transformation, which intersects with all the other pillars will arise from innovative future generations.

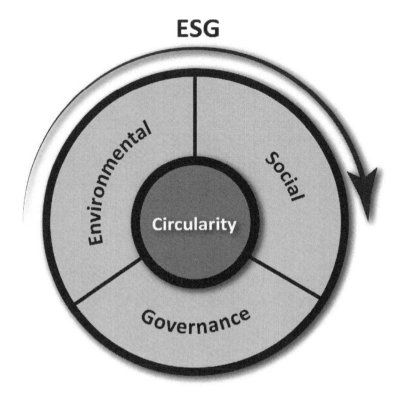

- Digital Transformation: The ability of data and the insights they generate from physical products, experiences, publications and media to deliver a new value proposition for investors, corporations and consumers alike.

- Environmental: Maintain air quality, reduce CO_2 emissions, and eliminate exposure to water contaminants, improve aging infrastructure systems, innovative technologies, and processes.

- Social: Protect and sustain human health, address water scarcity, stop child trafficking, end human right violations, ensure inclusion and diversity.

- Finance/Execution: Reducing costs, improving customer satisfaction, and creating greater societal value for generations, all while increasing stakeholder profits.

What makes this so important is that this raises questions about how we deploy money from either pension funds, or sovereign wealth funds, or government money, to actually creating public good, is an undervalued asset that gets into this whole sustainability conversation.

While the information contained in each pillar is currently not weighted the same in investment and corporate decision-making, Adriaens made another good point that the availability of new data measured through ubiquitous sensing and so-called data fusion (combining different types of data) will help with advancing the entire sustainability paradigm and the objectives of future generations.

What's more, this is creating an even deeper interconnected discussion on economic vitality and creating diverse and thriving communities for generations to come.

Stewardship Across Generations

Generational thinking can lead to strong corporate sustainability. Over the years, organizations that work to develop strong sustainability plans understand the long-term views and focus on stewardship across generations by encompassing profit, people, technology, and the planet. When it comes to getting everyone involved both socially and environmentally, engagement with all stakeholders requires a complete understanding of all the market objectives.

Corporate social responsibility has become widely known in business circles and among generative families. Corporate sustainability has gained more traction as a comprehensive theory, addressing business performance focused on action and behavior that in turn result in social and environmental impact. Simply, understanding corporate sustainability is recognizing a significant shift in the way companies think about environmental, social, and economic issues.

It's no wonder we are hearing more and more discussion about companies abandoning the notion that one singular definition for CSR is what makes these principles successful. Rather, to be effective, the best companies are creating their own action practices that are best suited for their employees and their suppliers. Each of these tactics vary widely based the teams that are deployed and the specific culture of each organization.

Companies can act on corporate sustainability by adopting long-term and short-term business strategies to match development goals. These goals can be based on definitions designed to increase the development, awareness, and the ambitions of the current and future organization. A truly sustainable organization has common traits that are known globally and in business.

When we are engaging in a conversation about sustainability we must talk about CSR. We are engaging in a discussion about how sustainability is impacting the local community, society, and how it is playing a critical role in preserving the environment in respecting, enriching, and promoting human rights, and in the development of ethical and moral values within the company.

When we see the role of CSR, we need to recognize the importance of the reputation and image of the company and its employees. This reflection impacts financial and economic performances and ultimately stakeholders see this channeling through the entire supply chain to all the partners. Ethical and moral values inside the company have consequences outside the company.

The reputation of companies will extend to products and services. Ultimately, ethical and social perceptions are increasingly putting greater pressure on the business and now ecosystem decisions.

A Green Shift

Back in the 1970s, Amory Lovins, energy advisor and cofounder, Rocky Mountain Institute, was espousing think green designs and business strategies, helping companies consider environmental challenges through a different lens. While some have labeled him a utopian dreamer, Lovins led the way on the ongoing energy debate.

During the past decade or so, there has been a paradigm shift in the way individuals and companies view their environmental purpose. A greater emphasis has been focused on environmental health, social equity, and economic resiliency of thriving communities for future generations. Sustainability has often been recognized as a three-legged stool of people, planet, and profits. But as companies and individuals became more enlightened and realize their part in contributing to the greater good for future generations, the 3Ps are being replaced with a new mantra.

A generational shift is emerging, reflecting long-term priorities and with it a new focus. McDonough and Braungart build on the work of Lovins insight with their book cradle to cradle: remaking the way we make things, 2002. In their book, they offer an alternative to the linear cradle-to-grave industrial model of extract, manufacture, use, and dispose of products.

The Cradle to Cradle duo suggest where at the end of their useful life, products should not be just thrown away, rather they are encouraging innovators to rethink their positioning about end of life products and repurpose them as part of new products. To date, many start-ups and well-established companies have shifted their thinking and implemented in recycled material ways such as Herman Miller, Steelcase, Ford, and Nike.

They contend conventional, expensive eco-efficiency measures that just aren't going make the grade for recycling or emissions reduction—or for protecting the long-term health of the environment. They insist our industrial products were not designed with environmental safety in mind; and as a result, there's no ability to reclaim the natural resources used to fully prevent ecosystem destruction from occurring.

Rather than trying to create a stop-gap measure, the duo suggests creating a new solution from the ground up that is both eco-friendly and cost-efficient. The authors have tested their theory at the legendary River Rouge Ford factory; and on their own in their book itself, which is printed on a synthetic paper that doesn't use trees.

Perhaps the biggest question that needs to be asked and answered globally: How can we change the way we consume modern-day conveniences to restore the natural ecosystem? The take-make-waste model has just been feeding the human desire for decades. Manufacturers feed our insatiable appetite to possess and own the latest and greatest gadgets, fashion, vehicles, you name it, all contributing to us sucking the air right out of Mother Earth.

When asked would you go without a digital cellphone, research shows 97% of people say no. They need to be connected. The desire to be socially engaged is so great, but at what expense to the environment? It's the same challenge the safety industry has when trying to get people to keep their eyes on the road and hand on the wheel when driving. Individuals cannot help themselves. Much like Pavlov's research shows the ding on a cellphone is so great, we feel compelled to react to the text or voice message.

The root problem is that we all own too many things. As a culture, why do we need to possess a myriad of things rendering all of the older ones obsolete and headed for the landfill? We can all take a step back and recognize that as a direct manifestation of so many industries we now have a plethora of things that are really polluting the environment. Once we begin looking at the ecosystems and the processes, we instantly recognize the incredible wealth that is generated in this throwaway economy. It also leads us to one essential question about our own personal views toward the circular economy and sustainability.

In an earlier chapter 3, we addressed climate change as the long-term shift in Earth's climate and weather patterns. Using its own climate models and statistical analysis of global temperature data, National Aeronautics and Space Administration (NASA) scientists admit most of the emissions of carbon dioxide and other greenhouse gases into the atmosphere are impacting global temperature.

NASA and the National Oceanic and Atmospheric Administration (NOAA) study of the Earth's global surface temperatures report shows that 2019 was the second warmest year since modern recordkeeping began in 1880. Looking further, 2019 temperatures only trailed those of 2016, continuing the planet's long-term warming trend. The last five years have been the warmest of the past 140 years. Curiously, NASA did not explain the blip in 2016.

It took almost a century of research to reveal that each decade is warmer than the one before. Dedicated global-surface temperature research monitoring only began in the 1800s, before that there's no data showing human-produced fluctuations in the Earth's history.

However, what the current data does show is the average global surface temperature jumped more than 2 °F (slightly above 1 °C) ahead of the late 19th century. Data reveals the last Ice Age was closer to 10 °F colder than the pre-industrial temperature.

As more and more debate, there appeared to be some consensus that carbon emissions were having an impact on the climate. We started to see NASA, NOAA, and other scientists pointing out that carbon emissions are having a warming effect on the environment. Familiar names like Svante Arrhenius, Guy Stewart Callendar, and Charles Keeling really started to explore emissions for raising the atmosphere's temperature. It was Keeling that was known for the Keeling Curve in the 1960s, using computer models consistently, showing a doubling of CO_2 to produce a warming of 2 °C or 3.6 °F within the next century that drew more interest.

However, a key development comes by research of Serbian astrophysicist Milutin Milankovitch on his theory relating to the Earth's motion and long-term climate change. Studying the Earth's temperature dating back some 600,000 years, Milankovitch developed a mathematical theory on how orbital variations such as eccentricity, precession, and axial tilt affected solar radiation levels. These periods of orbital motions have become known as Milankovitch cycles. All of his findings were published in his book *Canon of Insolation and the Ice Age Problem*, in 1941.

By the 1960s, tech advancements found in deep sea ice cores and plankton shells, which helped pinpoint periods of glaciation, corroborated his findings.

Again, as scientists looked at all these models—that were actually decades ago—the real challenge is determining who would prevail in understanding the climate change. Perhaps as intense was the day American Bobby Fischer became chess champion after defeating Russian, Boris Spassky.

Climate change is truly, remarkably complex. And for those that want you to think we are spiralling out of control, step back and take a deep breath. Temperatures have oscillated from warnings of an impending ice age to a steady increase in CO_2 for decades. We have been discussing this problem for more than 150 years.

Whether we believe CO_2 is the biggest contributor to climate change or global warming is really best left up to the world's leading scientists to advocate for in various reports and studies. But we also don't want to turn a blind eye to what is going on behind the scenes. We can't ignore hidden objectives of governments or politicians who wish to hide their agendas behind some thinly veiled smokescreen.

Today we are at a tipping point of exploring new business models that are three-fold: drive profitability, reduce waste, and restore natural ecosystems before the industrial revolution boom. Now as individuals, communities, and governments, we must all talk about what is "fake science," and is it really focused on "saving the planet," for the good of all the living species and its natural resources and how humankind must be an active participant and think and act differently.

Supply Chain

Let's go back to what we have learned so far. For every company that makes the investment in the circular economy, we are improving. It's no wonder that our take-make-waste habits have led us to this point where we are now the throw-it-away society.

A circular world makes companies more efficient and profitable over a linear, take-make-waste model. This thinking from producing new products that are recycled or remade, and not necessarily from virgin raw materials, but from those that are sustainable.

What's more, in recent years, uncertainty has plagued the supply chain. Many businesses recognize the impact of the supply chain from a global perspective and the challenge of its constant disruption. This includes disruption from the unknown start-ups.

Some of the biggest uncertainty is caused by events including the U.S.-China trade, the pandemic, and as the saying goes, constant future unknowns, like other trades routes.

The COVID-19 pandemic opened up some serious challenges in the global supply chain. One significant weakness has to do with the realization of how vulnerable we are when getting essential supplies and parts. Prior to the pandemic, only 28% of organizations had implemented circular design.

Supply chains are built on just-in-time inventory and distributed component sourcing. U.S. manufacturers recognized they needed to reduce their reliance on China, factory lockdowns, and logistics disruptions. What was once a way to deplete stockpiles might need to be revised.

Companies might need to build backup in inventory and have contingency plans. Leveraging IoT technology and making considerable changes, in global operations, is enabling enterprises to shift their weaknesses without causing dramatic harm to already established partnerships.

Part of the problem is that manufacturers relied on industry consultants and analysts who convinced them that JIT (just-in-time) processes would lead to the Holy Grail, but instead it led to a complete reliance on China suppliers. While this alone wasn't the sole problem, a lack of technology and production weaknesses revealed a considerable need for manufacturers to rethink their operations and to shore up their supply chains.

Improving resiliency in the supply chain is essential for maintaining sustainability and circularity, which ultimately means profitability. While improving resilience will not come cheap, it will require persistence, and a dedicated technology strategy. Supply-chain executives must understand a one-size-fit all approach will not work with achieving resiliency.

Now more than ever companies need to consider operational and strategic goals, all while gaining a competitive footing and strengthening agility. During this time of uncertainty where global tariffs and other geopolitical challenges continue to disrupt supply chains, it's essential to look to sustainability initiatives now more than ever.

New Beginnings

The world leaders are struggling with how to move from linear to circular at a global economic model. Even the European Commission has developed an action in an attempt to engage more stakeholders to work through their existing business practices.

For instance, what if roads could fix themselves? We have been learning about self-healing materials for years—both polymers' and concrete—that can repair their own cracks. We've heard of it for healing smaller things, but now we are seeing it incorporated into the things that matter most. We are even learning about self-healing rubbers that will change the automotive industry and deforestation. There are other self-healing infrastructure designs that will have significant environmental benefits being developed as well.

The first step in improving climate change begins with each country, organization, and citizen improving their carbon footprint. That means putting the right measures in place to help improve their activities to reduce the amount of GHGs, and specifically carbon dioxide emitted.

We are simply calculating by summing the emissions, resulting from every stage of a product or service's lifetime. This means the material production, manufacturing, the products use, end-of-life, and even re-use. Again, the sole purpose here is to consider a product's lifetime, or lifecycle, and calculating different GHGs that are emitted, including carbon dioxide (CO_2), methane (CH_4), and nitrous oxide (N_2O), all of which have the ability to trap heat in the atmosphere.

Let's consider for a moment the building industry. The energy associated with a building's construction and operating looks a little different between operational carbon and embodied carbon. Operational carbon is the carbon load created and released during the use of energy to heat and power a building—consider the mechanical and electrical systems. Now the embodied carbon is what is then released during the manufacturing, production, and transportation of our everyday building materials.

Looking at the CO_2 emissions, by sector, from the 2019 Global ABC report shed even greater light on the overall pollution problem. Current numbers reveal emissions at 31% for the building and construction industry as a whole (including building finishes, equipment, and infrastructure), building operations 28%; transportation 23%; building materials and construction (steel, cement, glass, etc.) 11%; and other 7%.

Looking at all of this, there is no question about the urgency to address climate change and why it is a starting to be a global agreement that we are creating irreversible climate disruption to our environment. Many have suggested net zero carbon emissions as a target for new construction, as an example.

Even Black & Veatch, an employee-owned engineering and construction company, is stepping up to reduce its carbon footprint with a net zero GHG goal by 2025.

Paris Agreement

The Paris Agreement is meant to strengthen the resolve of countries across the world to reduce the global temperature rise this century well below 2 °C above pre-industrial levels.

Perhaps again we need to take step back. In 2015, there was huge support of the Paris Agreement, vowing to attempt to limit the planet's warming to 1.5 °C (2.7 °F), attempting to go back to pre-industrial levels. Many nations were more than willing participants to improve the climate.

Today, however, some of these nations are discovering these targets are extremely ambitious. When it comes to moving the climate dial below 2 °C it requires not just transformational change, but a continual shift in thinking, a major shift from fossil fuels, and a commitment from all countries, something that is currently not happening.

When U.S. President Donald Trump was sworn into office as the 45th President of the United States, he was determined that America should withdraw from the Paris Agreement. President Trump said compliance with the terms of the Paris Accord created onerous energy restrictions on the United States and would cost the United States a loss of about $3 trillion in GDP (gross domestic product) and 6.5 million industrial jobs.

Whether you consider President Trump's decision to be reckless or brazen to withdraw from the Paris Agreement, his point was, it would never succeed. It was doomed to fail if other egregious polluters did not commit to climate change immediately.

In 2015, China had successfully argued that it was still a developing economy and it was for this reason it deserved developing nation status and should not have to share the same burden of curbing emissions as a developed nation whose pollution went unchecked for decades. China was granted the request and is able to continue to increase its emissions for another staggering 13 years under the accord. This only fueled the ire of the leader of the free world and confused other environmentalists.

China abruptly reversed its thinking in November 2020. It stated that as a world leader it is now pledging to lead by example, befitting a country that aspires to be a superpower.

All of this was coming at a time when the U.S. was transitioning leadership from then former President Trump to President-elect Joe Biden, who has said he will reinstate the United States in the Paris Agreement once he has taken office.

China will be allowed to build hundreds of additional coal plants. While under the restrictions of the accord, the U.S. must pull back on all construction of coal and new plants. India can also double down its coal production, (prior to COVID-19), through 2020.

Think of it: India can keep producing while most of the world must stop? What does that say about the elimination of U.S. coal production? Even Europe is allowed to continue construction of coal plants.

The United States officially removed itself from the Paris climate accord on Nov. 4, 2020. Some five years earlier, nearly 200 countries committed to combat the climate crises.

Although at the outset, Angola, Eritrea, Iran, Iraq, Libya, Sudan, Turkey, and Yemen, did not join, which is problematic for solving global climate change. Keep in mind Iraq, Iran, Kuwait, Saudi Arabia, and Venezuela are the original founding members of the Organization of Petroleum Exporting Countries (OPEC). The reason these facts play a pivotal role is the United States is still the largest oil consumer in the world followed by China, Japan, India, and Saudi Arabia.

The drum beats by environmentalists to reduce oil production and consumption are getting louder as the younger generation is taking notice and action with their checkbooks, insisting fossil fuels are polluting our air and contaminating our water. As the beating gets louder, we are hearing more cries for the world that shun our reliance on oil and to use renewable energy sources.

The most damning argument to date has been the burning of fossil fuels, especially all of the petroleum-based products, which is one of the primary causes of climate change. This is not to mention the oil industry has notoriously been linked to oil spills that have caused pollution at almost every level of the earth: air, land, and sea. What's more, environmentalists also complain that petroleum-based products, like plastics, pollute the environment at every level when they degrade in landfills and in the ocean.

Plastic products are composed of various elements such as carbon, hydrogen, oxygen, nitrogen, chlorine, and sulfur. Plastics are generally produced by the conversion of natural products or by the synthesis from primary chemicals generally coming from oil, natural gas, or coal.

There are those believers that say if companies, countries, and individuals can work together to solve common challenges like climate change and sustainability, we acknowledge we can set aside our differences for all our future generations.

While the accord might want to block the development of coal in America, the U.S. cannot just stop production. It must transition to a cleaner, more efficient production system in states like Pennsylvania, Ohio, West Virginia, and more.

The United States has not made a national shift to climate change at this point. Many leaders oppose making the move away from fossil fuels. Moving away from fossil fuels can be likened to turning a spicket off. It must be a journey to make a natural shift away from existing services and solutions.

Regardless of President Trump pulling out of the Paris Agreement, many global countries, companies, and organizations have continued to support the accord.

With that in mind, The Network for Greening the Financial System (NGFS), a collaborative effort, was created to green the financial system and improve the efforts of the financial community in achieving the Paris Agreement goals. Part of these goals are to monitor the financial industry's role in managing climate risks and explore the available options of mobilizing capital for green and low-carbon investments.

We've been talking about sustainability and environmental reporting for a couple of decades now from a stakeholder perspective. But the true origins of reporting materiality for the investor community is perhaps the most visual piece of information, when in financial reporting that an investor can actually see impact on the environment. We are talking data that reflects the positive and the negative impacts. Actually, there are a host of climate guidelines that need to be considered from how to measure, report, compare, and improve, and answer all the people questions and ethical decisions and everything in between.

However, if there is one really good thing to come from all of this it's clear the financial sector has taken green much more seriously. Some of the credit for the green awareness can be given to NGFS and the efforts it has led. In fact, the NGFS has already issued a report that addresses climate change and its remediation efforts with an ever-increasing focus on the macroeconomic issues that are facing financial institutions. The report proposes a greater focus reporting tools, including increasing transparency and integrating all this climate change data into economic models for enhanced capture and disclosure of forecasting and predicting.

Compiled by the NGFS group of experts on monetary policy and climate change, the report finds that climate change and its mitigation will increasingly affect macroeconomic variables essential to the conduct of monetary policy. It highlights the need for central banks to strengthen their analytical toolkits, integrating climate risks into their economic models and forecasting tools.

As I see it, as sustainability reporting increases and it becomes an integral part of everyday economic and financial analysis, it will only be a matter of time before you discover the real benefits of scale for green and a circular economy.

It's hard to believe the United Nations Framework Convention on Climate Change (UNFCCC) was already entrenched in discussion on climate change more than two decades ago when it came together in March 1994. In mid-November and December 2015, the UNFCCC was held in Paris in an attempt to draw up more support and curb global greenhouse gas emissions and climate change. For decades, the UN countries have been debating the increasing problem with no positive outcome. Even after the signing of the Paris Agreement in November 2016, only 197 countries agreed prior to the U.S. withdrawing its support.

Keep in mind under the UNFCCC, many global nations agreed back at its formation to stabilize GHG concentrations "at a level that would prevent dangerous anthropogenic (human-induced) interference with the climate system."

Those words—whatever they really mean to each individual—have proven to be very ineffective if you weigh them up against the recent ecosystems challenges and how globally the world has had to cope with droughts, floods, earthquakes, tsunamis, wildfires, extreme temperature fluctuations, loss of food production, and other unstable natural occurring events.

Heidi Roop, assistant professor of climate science at the University of Minnesota reminds us, just like the climate systems we are interconnected and complex. We have witnessed multiple events scaffolding a region or season. For instance, cool wet springs delayed planting, followed by dry summer conditions, and relentless late summer and autumn rain all together lead to a crop that can't be harvested or isn't nearly as valuable. These impacts cascade across systems. They have extreme implications for our food systems, communities, and ecosystems.

She gave further insights that suggested we look West at wildfire smoke carried by jet stream to our own backyards. Look North we see regions warming twice as fast as the rest of the world. Look East and South where oceans are warming coasts and are threatened by sea level rising and we are experiencing more devastating hurricanes.

What do we know? Daniel Vimont, professor in Atmospheric and Oceanic Sciences, and director of the Nelson Institute Center for Climatic Research at the University of Wisconsin–Madison for instance, explained the Midwest in the United States is getting wetter and warmer. Those are the facts. Looking specifically at the state of Wisconsin, he noted the state experienced 21, 100-year rainfall events in the last decade. The same climate pattern is occurring across the entire Midwest.

Climate science reveals what we can expect with climate change, as our atmosphere becomes warmer, it has the capacity to produce more storms that cause more rainfall, particularly, some of the largest storms, the 100-year, 500-year, and even 1,000-year events. If we continue to use Wisconsin as the example, Vimont acknowledged residents might see a doubling in frequency of 100 year/24-hour rainfall events by the middle of the century.

Even beyond flooding, there could be compound events. We see even more things where rain is interacting with other phenomenon such as warmer temperatures or frozen ground or rain or snow or changes in freezing rain. Which leads to new events that we are not accustom to.

These changes in extreme rainfall events affect us all in different ways. In urban areas even more rain and much more dramatic events can lead to sewer overflows and poor water quality that impacts the human health. Agricultural areas in the Midwest are also negatively impacted. It leads to enhanced runoff and erosion. This impacts agricultural productivity, water quality, and even access to emergency facilities. As one example, in Northern Wisconsin, extreme rain events have caused some rural communities to be cut off from emergency services. They negatively impact the native harvest and lifeways of the population.

Cities, communities, and ecosystems are very vulnerable and sensitive to natural events. It's for this reason that it's important to consider how a particular area will change or how vulnerable it will be and the greater the risk. Ultimately, risk is eliminated or even reduced by preventing climate change. Is that doable in this environment? Finally, it's important to explore reducing the sensitivity of the community. What particular species; what economic sectors; what infrastructure is in place to ensure future growth?

The ability to answer these points will determine the ultimate outcome and adaptation actions. The more sensitive a given area, the greater the exposure in risks to stopping climate change. The less susceptible the impacts of the climate action, the better the ability to take advantage of the opportunities.

Generative Family Companies

The hallmark of a generative family, or any company for that matter, is its resilience during times of joy and crisis. During the COVID-19 pandemic, the world witnessed many 100-year-old family businesses adapt and transform during the adversity of the pandemic. Some of the companies were able to adjust rapidly to the needs and crises and revamp their strategy. Others diversified and expanded into new markets, remaining as resilient and efficient as possible. We also saw many companies crumble under the pressure, unable to apply new principles and adjust to market conditions.

If there is one thing all companies have in common during a lengthy multi-decade period, it is that they have probably seen or experienced some form of transformation—some good, some bad, and some more troubling than others—but in the end, they all know what it takes to be part of a community that means withstanding the environmental challenges that are necessary to find new pathways for sustainable growth.

Large or small, these companies understand they must be involved in continual reinvention or they will find themselves in extinction like those of Easter Island. These companies rely on their family members and thus they are able to adapt and pivot. Companies that do not have family members must rely on the passion of their employees during times of crises.

It is this insight that has helped many of these generational firms ride out the warning signs that can derail the best of the best. Even the best companies sometimes can't anticipate the challenges of COVID-19; a stock market crash, the Great Depression—can knock them to them to its core.

However, many enterprises—construction, manufacturing, healthcare, retail—have shored up their businesses. While fear is understandable, they work with family, colleagues, and partners to avoid turmoil that sinks even the best companies. Rather, these companies look ahead and constantly review the external challenges that will create internal pain points.

These firms are not only trying to sustain and maintain continual growth during a pandemic, but they are also trying to address the bigger goals to help end poverty, inequality, inclusion, diversity, transformation, and environmental destruction. These challenges are really opportunities, and that is how these companies are not failing, but growing during crises.

The right companies recognize that finding passionate people who can carry the torch to move the company forward will disrupt and transform a company. People become the legacy and the technology and solutions are only the processes for how to enable the journey. They all help to strategize and minimize the unforeseen economic hurdles that are sure to make the road even more troublesome.

It's no surprise then that sustainability, climate change, resiliency, circular economy, and even corporate social responsibility are always part of the corporate mission and vision of a highly successful company. These are defined and mandated by the owners of the company or by the top executives of any publicly traded company. They have followed an impact thesis, all while taking what should be a common-sense approach to addressing a not-so-straightforward challenge.

All of these efforts must work in tandem to produce a positive ROI (return on investment). Generative families are then, a microcosm of a larger market system with employees, suppliers/partners, customers, community, and the environment. They enhance communities and the standard of living for everyone that lives in the community.

For instance, consider a company like Bechtel and the way management thinks about CSR, otherwise known as Corporate Social Responsibility. This generative family thinks of its contribution to the world from an operational perspective and that means asking, "what it is going to leave behind." It also requires projects to simply minimize negative impacts and enhance the positive ones.

According to Dennis R. Jaffe in his book, *Borrowed from Your Grandchildren, The Evolution of 100-Year Family Enterprises, February 2020,* there is a three-part resilience cycle in how generative families respond to change:

1. *Prepare/anticipate*: Even when they are not preparing for a specific change, the family expects and anticipates broad general changes such as the need to develop a new generation of family members or even prepare for a shift in customers or products. They notice early warning signs.

2. *Engage/decide:* As a change approaches, generative families gather to consider what it means. They engage multiple family members in and listen to differing points of view before they take action.

3. **Renew/new**: After the change, generative families do not go back to the way things were. They find a new a path and work to implement it. While they respect tradition, they ae able to let go of anything that is obsolete.

Generative families want to make an impact. Ask most of them and they will come straight out and tell you they are impressed by human effort and ingenuity. That is why they are so acutely aware of environmental and social initiatives, such as circular economy and sustainability. The thought of plastic drifting into the rivers and oceans—along the communities they live, shop, and pray—is very unsettling.

Case Study
Trane Thinks Sustainably

In 2020, Trane Technologies formed as a new company built from previous acquisitions of Thermo King in 1997 and Trane in 2008, two industry leaders known for innovation in product and sustainability commitments. As one company, Trane Technologies brings together the history, expertise, and climate commitment of both brands into one new organization focused on creating a sustainable future for our planet.

With a purpose of challenging the company and because of the world changing, Trane Technologies' 2030 commitments are a set of goals that impact all areas of the company's business from operations, supply chain, employee, community development, and governance. In order to help reach these goals, investments and resources were renewed or begun.

The Center for Energy Efficiency and Sustainability (CEES) is an integral part of the company's internal efforts to keep Trane Technologies on track to achieve its bold sustainability efforts. CEES works to ensure that all levels and functions of the organization are working in tandem and that they cascade to the internal teams. CEES also assists in creating awareness and ownership of sustainability goals and puts action into the hands of each employee so that together the company can meet the sustainability needs of future generations while meeting its business objectives.

Through CEES, Trane Technologies created a vision of interdependence between environmental, social, and governance (ESG) goals. One of the first big victories explained Ben Tacka, sustainability programs leader, came in 2013 when Trane Technologies put together a sustainability action plan and established conversations on governance and set environmental structures and practices.

From its initial plan, the company has been on a clear path to meet sustainability objectives. As a part of that mission Trane Technologies is determined to help customers reduce emissions by one gigaton by the year 2030. It also has an objective to be a carbon neutral operation and return zero waste to landfills by the same period. Globally Trane Technologies wants its emissions intensity to reduce by at least 35%. Another goal was a hefty $500 million investment in research and development (R&D) to ensure the company could live up to its commitments, promises that require partners, suppliers, and investment in refrigerants that are next-gen, low global warming potential.

By 2030, not only is the goal to be carbon neutral in its operations, but also to execute on all aspects of its strategy to "lead by example." Trane Technologies is investing in its operations to increase energy efficiency by 2030, with the transformation largely beginning now. The machination is to consume 10% less energy than it did a decade earlier: producing more, but using less, and focusing on conserving those resources.

Giving Back to Community

Ask owners of these companies and they will say they care about the community, the society, the residents, and the environmental decisions they are making every day and how those decisions impact the world around them. These are the decisions that will greatly impact the community to which they send their children to school and their playgrounds.

This is where their friends see them every Sunday coming out their place of worship, or where they go for a quick beer to watch their favorite sporting event. This is their community. They are sensitive to their reputations and how their decisions impact others. They care about the community, and as leading citizens they feel responsible to help the community thrive.

Going back to Bechtel, it understands it's not solely about the physical asset but being able to improve the enabling environment. Bechtel views sustainability as an opportunity to minimize negative impacts from its projects and enhance the positive ones. It also believes wholeheartedly in sustainability, which goes a long way when working within the communities it is developing.

For instance, Bechtel's project team has learned by working closely with the government leaders and local citizens, and by focusing on improving the environment, it has a greater chance of being invited back for future projects. Bechtel recognizes this is not a one and done investment. It needs to ensure that everyone is fully embracing each step of the project; including the customer, government, community, and themselves throughout the process. When Bechtel leaves behind a bridge, roadway, plant, airport, subway, harbor, railway, each project requires the team to examine how they are impacting the environment.

Bechtel has to ask the right questions upfront and recognizes as a sustainable company that means asking and answering the following questions: Is it biodegrading the environment? Is it reducing the community's access to their own clean water or biodiversity or ecosystem services? What is the water or biodiversity or ecosystem services after it leaves? Will its efforts marginalize local groups from an economic development standpoint, creating winners and losers because of the way it is being managed by the local content program?

While communities start to thrive, with more growth comes additional issues about what is happening and how to address those future concerns once Bechtel is no longer present. For instance, what if more nitrates and phosphates continue to leach from fertilized farm fields into the waterways when it rains or the snow melts into the groundwater overtime, how will the community address these issues?

A company like Bechtel understands the social and environmental impact of its decisions. It recognizes it must engage in a variety of collaboration efforts to minimize nutrient pollution down the road. The team must also understand the dangers of how eutrophication can lead to hypoxia ("dead zones"), causing fish to die and a decrease in aquatic life. Excess nutrients can cause HABs (harmful algal blooms) in freshwater systems and will not only cause wildlife disruption, but it will also produce toxins that are harmful to humans. It's more than just building walls; it's building a sustainable community.

Bechtel epitomizes this belief. It understands that its responsibility is not solely about the physical asset. Executives believe in sustainability. They recognize the importance of improving the environment and the living conditions for every resident.

By improving the environment, Bechtel's project team recognizes that this is not a one and done investment. It is setting the tone and connections for the community. Bechtel has left a legacy for future generations.

Case study
Cementing Its Future
Take concrete, as an example. Compared to other building materials in terms of embodied energy and CO_2 emissions, concrete has been the construction material of choice for buildings and infrastructure expansion for decades. However, concrete has also been known for its horrible high-carbon footprint due to the energy intensive generation of Portland cement (which generally is the most notable ingredient of concrete, mortar, stucco, and non-specialty grout). That's why emotions run high when talk of construction materials that

contain latent energy, and equally expended energy, in the production of those materials occurs.

Thus, in wake of an outpouring to address the demand for performance and sustainability, LafargeHolcim is working to reduce carbon emissions and shifting toward low-carbon construction. It is making a strong commitment to high-quality and sustainable building materials worldwide to introduce more sustainable products.

As the largest cement manufacturer in the United States, LafargeHolcim is making a plea to the construction industry to lower its carbon footprint. As part of this effort it is working with partners to leverage its own cementitious materials (SCMs) through its own EnvirocoreTM Series products, which include OneCem Portland Limestone Cement, MaxCem Blended Cement, and NewCem Slag Cement, which use byproducts from other industries that offer sustainability and performance advantages for those who construct buildings. Their use as a partial replacement for Portland cement not only results in more durable, high-performance concrete, but also lowers energy consumption and GHGs. For every ton of clinker replaced by SCMs, CO_2 emissions are reduced by approximately 0.8 tons.

While all products from the Envirocore Series benefit project performance and reduce carbon emissions, one product within this portfolio has the potential to be incorporated into a broad spectrum of applications: OneCem, its Portland Limestone Cement.

The good news here is that the OneCem has been rigorously tested to verify its concrete strength development, setting time characteristics, durability, and other performance properties. In the U.S., LafargeHolcim plants have produced more than 3 million metric tons of OneCem for concrete construction applications throughout the country.

LafargeHolcim is also focused on other energy saving approaches. In the U.S., it opened a new solar field next to its Hagerstown Cement Plant in Maryland. The solar array will provide clean, renewable energy for the facility's operations. LafargeHolcim's solar field, built in partnership with Greenbacker Renewable Energy Company, began operations in October 2020, and is expected to generate 10 MWac of energy on-peak, which should provide about 25% of the plant's annual requirements. More importantly, the solar addition will prevent the equivalent of roughly 12,375 tons of CO_2 emissions from entering the environment. All electricity produced by the solar array will be used by the plant during operations.

U.S. Green Building Council (USGBC), for instance, is stepping up its effort to build the value of builders and developers in implementing new approaches to design and plan a more inclusive world. This is an organization that is focusing heavily on providing a world that welcomes everyone by leveraging sustainability efforts through its efforts.

Through these efforts, cities and communities are building a more inclusive and sustainable vision for the future. Leadership in Energy and Environmental Design (LEED) is drawing a roadmap for creating high-quality, affordable housing that improves quality of life. Achieving LEED certification is an indication that a home meets the highest sustainability standards.

A LEED-certified home has a direct impact on decreasing utility bills by reducing energy and water consumption and providing a much healthier indoor environment by improving air quality and using materials that reduce our exposure to toxins and pollutants. LEED also provides a roadmap for creating high-quality, affordable housing that improves quality of life. This is something that many energy-aware residents pay attention too and even look for in a home.

Case study
Mining Sustainability
It takes a village. We've all heard that expression. In this case, it's more than true. It requires the support of the community and commitment from a dedicated group of technical, business training, and social development. This is not to mention it takes a whole lot of people working in concert to make a cooper mine come to fruition. Let's not forget all the environmental conservation, road safety, and much more stakeholder engagement, but we will get to that part of the story shortly.

Any company knows there are cash and social investments that it must go through during its stewardship programs. It's part of its CSR. For each company there are limits too depending on its goals. For a generative family business, the bigger pay back is what it is able to give to the community in all the processes it has engaged in. That means ensuring both short-term and long-term consequences are evaluated when making decisions for the local residents.

Even though generations change, Bechtel family values generally have remained consistent. It views business, society, and the environment as interdependent. The company continues to ask: Is what we do harmful to the environment? Are our employees treated fairly, and do they benefit from our prosperity? How do we deal with adversity? Do we punish our employees or are we loyal to them? What are the impacts? What are the opportunities? What are we leaving behind?

Consider this example: Las Bambas, a Greenfield copper concentrator project located at 13,780 feet (4,200 meters) above sea level in the Peruvian Andes. It is owned and operated by MMG, which has helped Peru further strengthen its position as the world's second largest copper producing nation, by engaging the local community as part of the discussion and really looking at the inclusion of different segments of that population.

As a contracting company, Bechtel actively partnered with MMG to provide engineering, procurement, and construction services, to successfully hand over the project in 2015. Thanks to its 140,000 tonnes per day concentrator, the mine produced more than 453,000 tonnes in 2017, its first full year of commercial production, becoming one of the world's 10 largest copper mines. In fact, this mine represents 2% of all the world's copper production today.

In addition, all of Bechtel's efforts are based on the funds coming from the customer. If the customer is not providing the necessary funding, Bechtel can only produce a final product based on what it negotiates for the community. In this scenario, Bechtel was really working to engage everyone in the community. The Bechtel team admits it had to be extremely creative and sensitive to the needs of everyone.

Bechtel's Global Head of Sustainability Tam Nguyen explained engaging a lot of the local businesses into the work to provide a range of services (i.e. transportation, hotels, housing, food services) made all the difference. Bechtel works in advance of a project to get the communities involved so it can begin working with them to provide training and teaching them different management competencies, such as purchasing goods and services. Bechtel also invests time in working with hotels to upgrade all of their safety and health and hygiene features not only for workers, but also so that they can attract tourists.

That means connecting local communities to direct employment opportunities, Bechtel created some 5,000 jobs and conducted 24,000 hours of training for positions such as surveying and earthworks. Bechtel is not only engaging the community into contracts, but it is also building capacity.

Bechtel knows at the start of every project it will decommission, finish its operation, let's say, in about two years, and then move on to the next project. But in the process, it will work with the communities to help them adjust, transitioning away from the project so that it doesn't create a "big boom and bust."

Nguyen draws attention to the fact that Bechtel wants to build up the communities, so they can self-perform from the revenue they are generating.

Each new business venture is creating value for Bechtel all while paving the way for a more prosperous community with better roads, bridges, industrial facilities, and also better internet infrastructure.

All in all, Bechtel's mission is to focus on creating and developing comprehensive sustainability management system of procedures, programs, tools, and plans that enable the project and the community to function long after the initial project team leaves. This involves conducting workshops and helping local residents understand the impacts and how to best manage them, including conflict prevention and recycling programs.

The Microsoft Way

Take another company, Microsoft that works with its own employees and ISVs. The company is deeply supportive of its team and encourages all partners to be participatory in the ecosystem. It doesn't view social and environmental impact as an add-on, peripheral set of actions, but as part of the core strategy. It believes in encouraging its employees, and ISVs, in establishing a core set of values and skills to solve the social and environmental issues they care about and create the methodologies to drive company growth and deep social change.

Walton, manufacturing industry executive, Microsoft acknowledged the younger generation is coming to the realization and have a need to be active and they must participate. They have a unique ability and society needs to encourage them to create change.

He believes it is happening. Today's youth are at a point that possibilities abound for them. If a company really wants a new group of employees, they need to inspire them to be the creators of change—to be given the guidance and inspiration to understand the groundbreaking opportunities that lay ahead. Walton said younger people are at a stage where possibilities are everywhere and they want to be actively engaged.

The vast majority of young people are interested in the human component and humanity. They still have the belief they can reshape and redesign our thinking for the betterment for each other. Walton noted the reason the Baby Boomers struggle with the Millennials is they want to be "won over and brought to manufacturing."

At its simplest, manufacturing is all about achieving sustainability goals and that means shifting investments to tap into new opportunities. That's means shifting perceptions of the industry itself. Many younger people view manufacturing as environmentally destructive and as a dying industry compared to the more exciting industries they begin their career in.

As Baby Boomers ready for retirement within the next five to 10 years, many manufacturers have failed to prepare to create a strong sense of identity with the next generation of leaders. Manufacturing as an industry failed to frame itself around a shared history and a sense of purpose driven by core values and competencies. Rather it pigeon-holed itself around a bunch of salacious videos of iron workers or laborers, sweltering in the heat, trying to make flour in a plant.

What the industry should have spent more time on, Walton explained, was educating the next generation about all the aspects that are needed to run a manufacturing operation. Millennials for example, needed to see up close how manufacturers pursue growth with a systematic mindset. Manufacturers based all of their activities, as investors, business leaders, and agents of social change, building off of each other.

As Microsoft's Sam George, VP of Corporate IoT Azure, has suggested on more than one occasion, manufacturers are compelled by a strong sense of identity, framed around a shared history and a sense of purpose, guided by core values and intense competencies all focused on a common goal.

In his view, manufacturers are like a generative family—they live, work, and play in their community and have roots that are deeply interconnected. They are proud to be part of the big infrastructure projects that make the company grow. To grow, we need the trust our employees, customers, partners, and the entire supply chain.

Articulating a great sense of confidence and seeing the humanity in manufacturing is how our younger generation will aspire a career in manufacturing. This great influence is what has been missing in U.S. manufacturing and perhaps in manufacturing in general.

Walton noted some Millennials are seeing the impact of what some of their peers are already accomplishing in manufacturing. They've already witnessed change happening in a manufacturers' product line and not being able to just demand it. These are real sustainability impacts.

These changes are impacting and restoring the natural environment. They are helping manufacturers reduce less waste, design better projects, and make more money for the shareholders along the way.

Walton pointed out these are changes to the way manufacturing is approaching its efforts and Millennials are demanding it today and, oh by the way, they are getting their way, too!

Going Global

When looking at the bigger picture, it's essential to consider both a macroeconomic and microeconomic perspective when transforming developing countries into more prosperous nations. With the help of these companies and their continued involvement, emerging nations can continue to develop their economies and political background of their countries and their overall strategies.

Here is another example. Family-owned business, Warp + Weft has made a pretty impressive impact on the apparel industry, selling almost 500,000 pairs of jeans.

It says it has saved almost 893 million gallons of water in the process. During the past three decades Warp + Weft has focused on regenerative design approaches, responsibly sourced cotton, eco-friendly dye, mastering water-saving techniques that require less than 10 gallons to make a pair of jeans—which as we can all imagine helps each of us in the community and the environment.

The company also goes to great lengths to emphasize that it avoids the environmentally harmful bleaching process by opting for cutting-edge Dry Ozone technology, making it fully compliant with international social and environmental & quality standards.

Taking a plant tour in person has not been doable, but it is possible to take a virtual tour, and once you watch the movement, it truly is a one-stop-shop cutting, stitching, wet-dry processing that turns something so small into your new very comfy, favorite pair of denim jeans.

The most proactive and tenacious companies, governments, and individuals will encapsulate circular-economy principles into their environmental sustainability. Transformation begins with adopting design thinking and managing risks to identify, quantify, prioritize, and analyze all the data for a greener and more digital tomorrow.

CHAPTER 5

FUTURE

Grey to Green

The world needs to move from grey to green, fueled by design techniques that are sustainable in a circular economy. This movement needs to be invigorated by the next generation of innovators who are committed to circularity and sustainability. No longer can we hear the rhetoric about climate change. We need the support of all industries, government, cities, and individuals to achieve our common goals.

But here we are right now. As a society we are at a crossroads that will determine the future for generations. One fork leads to continued environmental destruction. The other fork leads to taking responsibility for our individual actions for ignoring decades of wasteful behavior in a make-take-waste world. Restoration is long overdue to the devastating destruction we have caused to our natural environment. Every government, city, and individual must decide which fork in the road to take to determine the outcome for future generations.

The truth be told, late renown Australian scientist and professor Frank Fenner had even predicted humans will most likely be extinct within 100 years as a result of overpopulation, environmental destruction, and climate change. If you want to know his credentials, well, he helped eradicate smallpox. And he's already 10 years into the prediction he made in 2010.

Fenner based his assumptions on a few points: The consuming public has unbridled consumption coupled with the massive human population predicted to be 8.5 billion people by 2030. Even further, the United Nations has projections of 9.7 billion people by 2050 and 11.2 billion by 2100; and this is across all countries.

Not to disagree with an eminent scientist of Fenner's caliber, but at this point anytime we say something is not reversible that is a bit too pessimistic, especially when we talk about the future and opportunities for young innovators. As Fenner saw it, it was too late to reverse the damage that had been created since the Industrial Revolution. As already discussed, that is where all this Anthropocene has all begun and that is why it is so imperative global unity must begin its work. He predicts the world population will experience the same fate of Easter Island. Other scientists have concurred that we have just 100 years before we see massive mayhem to our natural ecosystem.

This is where science and humanity come together. If humankind sees the world differently, change will occur. We need to move past our sterile societies of building massive stone statues and demagogues. It's not about giving up; it's about forging forward and readjusting our thinking and doing so for future generations.

Most people remember VHS (video home system), which was a very popular linear system for playing videos and movies until DVDs (digital versatile discs) came on the scene. This, of course, was long before streaming services, like Netflix and Hulu. VHSs had become so popular that by the last time a VHS movie was produced in 2005, there were 90 million machines still playing VHS tapes. Just think of how this contributes to all the waste we have been discussing.

The point here is that consumers purchased their movies or rented them from the now defunct brick-and-mortar store like Blockbuster and watched them on their home systems. At the time, most people didn't have the environmental benefit of streaming versus buying a video like they do today. However, today, we have the option to rent so many things in the circular economy, such as scooters, bikes, cars, and homes.

We have the option to consider, if we live in it, we should preserve it. We need to continue to increase our resilience and our future cooperation as a society. There are those who question the science around the need for action. Perhaps the point here is not to persuade people on the science facts. More importantly, we need to convince them on climate, but to get everyone to agree that we need to work together to regenerate the destruction that has been created to our ecosystems since the Industrial Revolution. It's a start. Think of it this way, if we can all contribute toward restoring the natural ecosystems, and at least have this common goal—we can move from grey to green in our land, seas, and air.

Net Zero Awakening

Pressure is mounting every day for more and more companies and countries to recognize this is a Decade of Action. As the clock ticks down, governments, businesses, and individuals are quickly awakening to the need to achieve net-zero emissions.

We have all heard that even China has made a new declaration to the world to commit to respect circularity and sustainability. That's a huge step if every other country also honors their sustainability commitments for a cleaner and greener world.

Talking Terms

So, let's review what comes to the forefront when talking about net zero. Simply, we are eliminating the greenhouse gas (GHG) emissions, especially carbon dioxide. The goal is to get at or near zero. Another term commonly used is carbon neutral. And some companies are even targeting what they are calling carbon negative. These companies are considered carbon negative when they eliminate more carbon than they emit each year. That means they have proven they can go beyond what is required and are having an even greater impact.

For a final set of technical terms here, carbon neutral is sometimes referred to as carbon neutrality, the action of removing carbon dioxide from the atmosphere, as much as is put into it. Oftentimes in the same sentence you will hear people use the words zero carbon and that is where much of the science debate comes into play. But for the moment let's just stick with trying to be better global environmental citizens for this discussion.

Microsoft has stated it is seeking to be carbon neutral and has set a target date by 2025. As part of that goal, it has stated it plans to shift to 100% supply of renewable energy. In addition, its entire vehicle fleet will be electric. This is certainly a bold position for the company, which has also invested $1 billion to help restore Mother Earth and achieve eco-friendly objectives.

Microsoft has loudly rung the bell with many customers with its Transform to Net Zero program in an effort to offer to help them make the journey. Many companies are already participating such as: Nike, BP, Starbucks, Unilever, Mercedes-Benz AG, A.P. Moller, BSR, Danone, Shell, MasterCard, AT&T, T-Mobile, SK Telecom, Ministry of Education, University of Notthingham, European Parliament, Nestle, Mark & Spencer, PepsiCo, Farmlands, Land O'Lakes, EcoLabs, Beierdorf AG, to name a few.

In the simplest of terms what this means is removing as much carbon in the atmosphere as is put into it. Think about a building with solar panels that sends renewable energy to the grid that is equal to the amount of energy taken out that is net zero. Many companies and countries are striving for 2030 as the target. Others have a more ambitious goal of 2025, and yet still others have set 2050 as the final mark for completion. Regardless of the deadline, there seems to be a growing consensus that the carbon emitted into the air can be reduced and it's time that everyone contributes to fix the problem that has been created across the globe.

Essentially for countries and cities to go net zero this will require significant changes to lifestyles. For the sake of this discussion, let's consider net zero in relation to what is being used in a building. If the building is working at net zero energy that would mean that it is producing as much or more energy as it is using. The total amount of net zero energy used by the building on an annual basis is equal to or less than the amount of renewable energy (energy created by sources that are naturally replenished, such as wind or solar) created on-site.

Keep in mind a net zero building is usually connected to the grid and can sell excess power, as well as purchase that additional power during times of high energy demand. Remember, things change due to weather, and over the course of an entire year, this building will be net zero because it cleanly produces as much energy as it consumes.

Therefore, if a net zero building is one that consumes only as much renewable energy as it produces on-site, a net zero energy building is one that cleanly produces all the energy it consumes on-site, no waste. So, if we understand all of this again, we must have the data to track all the man-made emissions, and that is where cloud tools, AI, and machine learning provide much-needed visibility into the process.

It's important to make sure not to confuse the term zero carbon with the aforementioned. This term describes when there is actually no presence of carbon and thus none was produced in the first place.

Companies of all sizes, from all industries and countries are stepping up to the plate and taking sustainability seriously and putting nature at the center of their efforts by focusing on carbon, water, waste and biodiversity, land, and soil.

While achieving sustainability objectives isn't an easy task. That is why if you have been paying close attention, you know the United Nations has a campaign called Race To Zero, pushing its carbon goals on countries, governments, and businesses in the hopes the world will unite for sustainability.

Build Better by Design

Sustainability starts with design. We must think more circular and eradicate the traditional linear thinking of make-take-waste. We must all start with the premise—for any industry to succeed — design must be at the core. We must build it better from the beginning.

Sustainable design in a circular world begins by observing natural ecosystems and learning how well people adapt and creatively make products to meet their material needs. Design with intent. Design with a purpose. Design begins observing people in the natural ecosystem and learning how they will adapt to the environment to meet their needs.

We do not want another Easter Island. We do not want history to repeat itself since we have discovered how we have been destroying our ecosystems. Rather we want to leverage design in a more efficient way to work, to build our world, and to view the data to meet our demands.

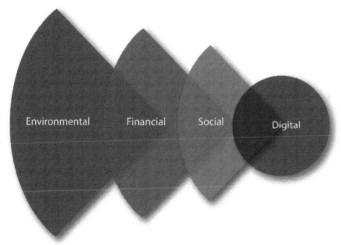

It's gathering insights to create products customers expect and may want. It is imperative we create efficiency gains. This means constantly looking at service of life and understanding all the compulsions of the customer from the farm, to the fork, at the retail store, and at the factory. It's complete discovery at all levels—local and global.

It's not about extraction. It's about constantly sparking new ideas and services into everything we do. We need to always consider how we can make our world more sustainable for our children, their children, and their grandchildren. That means using the least amount of material and offering the best product or service possible. What we have learned over time is that not everything has to be based on a physical product. This leads us back to our rent vs. own debate.

Rather than own, in this new model, we are sharing products over and over again. Airbnb, for instance, was created when two designers had some space to share and hosted some guests looking for a place to stay. Today millions of people use the Airbnb platform to book travel accommodations across the globe. Again, do you need to own a travel home, or rent one out?

We are also seeing the move away from more stuff, as streaming services come online from the likes of Netflix, Apple, HBO, and Disney+ growing in popularity and we abandon owning fewer physical things like DVDs and BluRays. While this is all better for our ecosystem, are we really getting on board with the idea of owning less or even embracing the concepts of repurposing and reusing products all with the good intention of saving the environment?

Perhaps the question comes down to how do you provide value to your customers? Or can you provide value to your customers using a minimum amount of material? The real answer is how do you service your customer? Consider Tarkett DESSO, a flooring company that has cut waste and reduced its consumption of virgin material by treating old carpet as a valued commodity. By leveraging Cradle to Cradle principles with its ReStart program, the company is able to collect carpet from its customers, and other sources, and removes the fibers from the backing. The EcoBase backing is 100% recyclable. The returned carpet is processed through the firm's recycling facility, which separates the yarn and other fibers from the backing and is then used as an ingredient in roads and roofs.

We all recognize that stuff happens, and people are not perfect, but we have a moral obligation to use the tools at our disposal to assure we have the best interest of future generations. If the design process is not linear, we need to ask ourselves why are we making our products linear?

As time goes on, this will extend to every device, tool, and piece of equipment that comes to mind and we will ask ourselves do we really need to own that? Thus, today ride-sharing and home rentals have become big business and people are doing it more and more for ecological reasons. These companies have successfully transformed a product-oriented approach into a service platform.

Once we all look at our ecosystems as being essential to everything, we will stop taking and wasting and will be looking to designing and regenerating.

Time and time again people say we have to move away from charging for physical things and services, because it's inherently wasteful, versus charging for time, which is what people most value. Here's the question: If we believe this excess is bad for our environment and intrinsically destructive, not to mention wasteful, why do we all still do it?

We know we use goods. Many people like nice things. Most of which they have to purchase. And they contract for services because they want to enjoy their time. Here's the thought, let's up the ante and charge for that time. In the process, companies make more money by using less resources from the Earth.

Let's focus more resources on the service. Rather than focus on making more things, how about greater emphasis being placed on the quality of the things we make and improve the training and the service? Customize it. Charge for time and get rid of the production to fix broken, extra stuff. Factories will make more money because they are making better goods and providing better services. Supply chains will be enhanced because we are not clogging them up.

Less items will be broken and destroyed, and we can focus on the service of delivery and not just the speed. And, as a means of differentiating and growing our business, we will happen to get less waste almost as a byproduct. Less products overall will be shipped, meaning less corrugated cardboard and similar dunnage will be required, reducing what ends up in landfills.

Perhaps another point we might want to consider is how to improve and protect items that ship in general. Rather than increase package material by some 40-70%, which again just adds to more waste in landfills as most are not reused. A final note here for shippers, perhaps it's time to evaluate the 36-inch drop equivalent. Time to bring in better connected rails to stop and sense when a package is about to hit the floor, causing damage. The large amount of returned customer product is destined for landfills, proving once again costly, wasteful, and certainly not sustainable by any measure.

IoT, Digital Twin, and AI

When we talk about saving the world, we can't continue this discussion without addressing the elephant in the room: technology. The first question everyone asks is which solution should I use? Perhaps the best way to address that question is to answer with the father of time management, Peter Drucker, who stated, if you can't measure it, you can't improve it. So, it's all about the data. But perhaps we need to look at it more collectively: we can't change, what we can't measure.

When we think about digital transformation, we are bringing the best of both worlds together. Sam George, VP, IoT Azure, Microsoft, has told me repeatedly, the first thing he always counsels a customer on is to examine what's really at the core of their business and if we had the ability to know something, faster or in realtime, what could we do with that? Even more importantly, how would we leverage that data? He explained this is where the IoT journey typically starts with executives simply monitoring, analyzing, improving, and ultimately transforming businesses.

The most important thing George noted is to always get companies to start small and work incrementally. He reminded me how often he works with companies again and again, and that companies that do this really well take a high value, yet relatively straightforward item they are connecting in their business, find insights from that, and drive real business results.

Ultimately, this gives them the confidence to move on to that next turn in the digital feedback loop and that is where you wind up with rampant enhancements in businesses. Exponential improvements in businesses don't happen from a big moonshot that takes a couple of years and then at the end of it have some great solutions. It happens from incremental solutions that build on themselves and become better and better through the through digital representation.

Data needs to play a critical role in how we help regenerate the natural ecosystem. Data needs to be in a form that we understand. It needs to be in a format that benefits the user, and that the user has the skill to understand the data. That is what sustainability is all about. Historical data analysis must keep pace with the trends and continue to add necessary contextualized insights.

Currently we are suffering from translation gaps. We need to create the public and private partnerships that reduce these gaps around the world and protect the information that is useable and sustainable for growing better crops and feeding the world. This includes creating the transparency that intersects with the credibility for the data so that buyers and sellers are able to track all the data from dirt to fork.

Also, leveraging robust analytics gleaned from AI-driven systems is putting decision-making information from renewable energy sites in front of the right people at the right time.

If we want sustainable cities, and therefore if we want businesses, cities, governments, and individuals to be good eco-friendly citizens, then we need to understand the constant journey of change. That is why digital transformation simply means a digital journey. Digital transformation is about change, but really big change. Perhaps much bigger than Baby Boomers can truly embrace. We need to have our natural environments constantly talking with our oceans and species because as humans we are constantly changing and evolving generationally, some have even called it a social utopia that we need to dramatically readjust our high-tech cities.

Technology also needs to keep up pace to solve the growing challenges. Thus, the best way to understand and to meet your needs for this rapid digitization is to consider this as a constant journey to sustainable enlightenment with design at the core. Ultimately, strangers are connecting to strangers and even high value, yet relatively straightforward items, or connecting to something in business that drives real business results. These actions then give the confidence to move on to that next turn with rich semantic modeling and that is where you wind up with exponential improvements in businesses.

The first step is measure. Measure what's important to you. You can't improve if you don't measure. It's critically important to always review the necessary data. You must have a plan and stick to the sustainability goals.

It's about always having sustainability as part of everything you do and measuring those efforts in order to start improving and seeing real tangible results. For instance, one industry that is gaining in significance is packaging sustainability. There are many challenges in the food industry and it's imperative that food manufacturers conduct a complete analysis of all threats and opportunities for business prior to the process of selecting goals and projects. This includes evaluating a sustainability strategy that will help to examine corporate goals that meet consumer objectives and adhere to the natural resources in the meaningful course of conducting business.

Tools like the IoT, edge computing, AI, and the cloud all come together to provide that measurement, visibility, and those breakthrough insights companies need to move to the next level of success.

Targets and objectives are critical. Organizations, cities, people, all learn the need for goals purpose-built for success.

That is how globally the world will hit its green mission and move to the next target phase. Business outcomes need to align with environmental ones. When a level of success is obtained, organization sets will move circularity forward. Once the goal is set, we all become better corporate citizens. That is how we continue to evolve using digital transformation.

Let's look at a candy processing production plant, as another example. While it's great to have many different data points, the key is to have data that will lead to the breakthrough insights that would help them optimize it and achieve sustainability goals. Measuring lots of things might seem important, but at the end of the day, it comes down to only needing a couple data points. By casting a wide net, this company found it only needed a small subset of that data that was really critical to optimize its production. Sometimes it actually works the reverse way too, where businesses measure a lot of things and then find they need to be more sustainable in other areas as well.

Digital Twin and Cities

When we think about sustainability in the digital age, there are many intersecting circles of information and insights that impact all socio-economic demographics, including those that lack access to the internet or banking opportunities.

The deployment of IoT (internet of things) and digital innovation is a major driver behind this wealth of big data.

The growth of sensors integrated into energy, water, transportation, and housing infrastructure, for example, informs how emerging incidents are detected, appropriate personnel is notified, and then activate various smart systems within the infrastructure to react and mitigate the impending situation.

Tomorrow's connected cities will use ubiquitous sensing to analyze information and make better, quicker decisions about environmental conditions. For example, as technology is deployed to meet low-emission and zero-emission standards, sensors will monitor and communicate equipment performance and identify where problems arise.

With IoT connected to all aspects of a city's infrastructure, a city will become more resilient and adaptive to climate change, energy and water needs, traffic congestion, and the broader human experience by monitoring usage, failure, needs for upgrades, and being responsive to social needs.

Cities have to think about energy in the digital age like it's a virtual power plant. Every physical asset consumes energy and produces emissions, depending on use and its design. What was once considered a stationary piece of infrastructure becomes a data streaming asset. A car is thought of as a sensor on wheels. An energy plant is a digital database of operational knowledge. As a result of collecting so much data from these infrastructure assets, and the way the data is being collected, the definition of infrastructure is becoming broadened. It is not just the concrete and the steel, but it's also the whole digital twin.

So, every infrastructure has a digital twin. And the digital twin is essentially made up of all the data, information, and the insights on that system. And while still in the very early stages this is going to be a major transformation in how we think about all the assets around us. It replicates all that is happening.

The IoT, artificial intelligence (AI) used to extract insights from data, and the cloud as a storage, data processing and distribution medium are linking the physical and digital worlds by altering every single function within smart factories, smart cars, smart meters, agriculture, videos, manufacturing, you name it, and it's getting connected. Long gone are the days of making the same product for everyone.

Today it's all about using data for customization. As new levels of connectivity, advanced computing, smart sensors and devices, and improved data access/storage increase the breadth, volume, and resolution of available manufacturing data, manufacturers need to use this data to design better in a circular economy.

As the world continues to evolve, manufacturers and businesses will continue to become smarter and more data centric, converting the digital twin at more and more operational scale. The true power in the IoT and AI is only just beginning, as business revamps in massive process facilities and industries, but also for thousands of mid-tier industries that are seeing the power to use economies of scale to design less waste.

We are in the midst of witnessing manufacturers outfit their operations to make less waste, because it makes sense from a cost and efficiency perspective. Companies of all sizes will need to design and create knowledge-based systems on digital models of their entire environments from buildings, factories, farms, streets, stadiums, health equipment, your name it. It's all about creating better products, optimized operations, and reducing costs, upping the customer experiences, and, of course, cutting out waste.

To achieve the promise of change at every function in their business for the better, it requires a real commitment to a new wave of innovation, differentiation, and productivity for the masses and giving back to the environment in the process.

Companies that take the right steps now will be in a position to transition each phase of the operation and continue to grow from early stage, through testing and implementation, and outward educational phases.

Crossing the IoT chasm to circularity requires a dedication to understanding ESG and using the data to make the leap forward. Creating a plan is more than saying you have a plan. It requires investing in it and applying IoT to the manufacturing operations for circularity at the design stage.

Many companies have built strong business cases, but it requires building a case that leverages a design model for circularity. That means moving away from what's been a linear make-take-waste approach to designing a new process from the ground up.

Achieving and exceeding ROI (return-on-investment) goals for long-term projects that give back require initial thinking and design. Building business cases is a must for manufacturers readying themselves for the IoT. It's all about building better products and creating optimal operations that create better customer experiences.

Using digital twin IoT for design products, for instance, will prove essential for the next decade, coupled with AI and machine learning insights if there is any hope to achieve the UN's sustainable development goals (SDGs). The IoT will have such a significant impact on public and corporate strategy and determining the tone of that conversation.

Smart leaders will look to the IoT to raise a broad set of new strategic choices about how value is created and captured; it often requires a whole new set of thinking. We will continue to see more grass roots changes, as the younger generations takes over leadership positions and engage the entire organization in embracing design/model thinking driven by sustainability.

For each company making the technology investments to achieve sustainability goals, organizations will look to create new IT (information technology) and OT (operational technology) thinking.

For some firms this might be integrating the IT and OT environments to optimize overall business processes. For others it might be to enhance information for better decisions. And then in some cases it just might be to reduce costs, lower risks and shortening project timelines. Regardless of the reasons, in the end, tapping the skillset of all these innovators will help to develop environmentally sound products faster and make companies ultimately more competitive.

Perhaps the other key point that should be made is don't get lost in acquiring old technology for the sake of acquiring. While preparing for the rapid surge (like what has happened during COVID-19) is requiring companies to acquire to stay competitive, keep in mind you are acquiring old linear solutions that are only putting a band-aid on a long-term problem.

Unless you have a strategic plan to transition to circular and lifecycle design quicker as a service company, you might be headed for prodigious headaches than you planned for in the long run. Simply, short-term gain, long-term nightmare.

In other cases, acquiring innovative companies to addressing corporate skills gaps related to IoT software technology and making internal changes to foster innovation and creativity is a feather in a company's cap. Now is a perfect time for big investment and rapid change.

Case Study
Living on the Red Sea

Consider for a moment the story of NEOM and living on the Red Sea. NEOM is the land of the future project that is being built on Saudi Arabia's Red Sea coastline as a living laboratory to break all barriers for innovation. While the concept for an advanced lifestyle is not new, it requires a complete understanding of economic viability, sustainability, productivity, carbon sequestration, biodiversity, erosion control, social, and technology.

Anticipated to accommodate more than one million people, NEOM, which means new future, will accommodate those who want to thrive by helping to develop and build a new model for sustainable living, working, and prosperity. This unique development will encompass towns, cities, ports, enterprise zones, research centers, sporting and entertainment arenas, and tourist destinations by the end of the decade.

NEOM, which means new future, is the vision of Crown Prince Mohammed Bin Salman and is part of Saudi Arabia's 2030 Vision to diversify and develop the Saudi economy and to play a leading role in global development. As we all know, the Saudi economy was built on oil. While NEOM is being spearheaded and initially funded by Saudi Arabia, its ultimate objective is to be funded as an international projective that will be led, populated, and funded from entrepreneurs all over the world.

This entire community seeks to embrace cultural diversity, as well as look to step outside the boundaries of cultural norms.

Some might even go far as saying this sustainable community will be more progressive, since it will be completely entrenched in digitization in every aspect of living.

A desalination plant has already been built on the land, which is converting 50,000-meters cubed per day from the sea to drinking water. For NEOM, its sustainability mission is clear: s topping pollution and extracting water from the ground so that in the future, it can return water to the surface. This is a renewable energy that is generating energy from wastewater in a sustainable way so that the cost of water is zero.

These are just some of the data points of the highly advanced renewable energy system in NEOM. It will support smart networks to improve performance and effectiveness of electrical networks, and other sustainability programs. The new land of the future will depend on information and that means leveraging big data, AI, and the cloud for the next decade, establishing a plethora of standards of community.

Decade of Action

Everything starts with getting the younger generation involved. We must inspire each child to be excited about Mother Earth. If the younger generation is not concerned about the ecosystem, how can society make it better?

This brings to mind a conversation I had with the late Jack Welch, who at the time was CEO of General Electric. Welch was discussing how every initiative started out with a smaller idea and how important it was to have good leaders who ignite passion. His words to me were continue to "kick-ass."

Alexandria Ocasio-Cortez used those same words to describe her vision of resolve for Millennials today. I was in my twenties when I met Welch, and when I read his book, *Jack Straight from the Gut*, in 2001, when he wrote how he encouraged all of the leaders he put in place who had the courage to, "kick ass and break glass."

As noted in Chapter 2 about Generations, perhaps the real key is understanding the desire and needs of each generation. We need to start to encourage the younger generations to be inspired and to see hope for the future, not darkness.

One Step Ahead

Today's businesses face many challenges in terms of what lies ahead with corporate social responsibility and sustainability. Businesses large and small are required to keep pace with new initiatives. That means staying ahead of the technology curve and, even more importantly, all the rules and regulations on a wide array of social, CSR governance, ESG, stakeholders, generational, and partnerships that are contributing to enhancing the quality of life for our natural ecosystems.

Understanding these indicators is not a matter of if, but when. Thus, recognizing credible signs to play your part in

CSR and the quality of life among a plethora of generations is a moving target.

That is why no one approach will work. Each corporation will have to think differently about the way each generation views its quality of life in relation to work, health, and environment. Some companies will need to transform their corporate responsibility efforts to meet the growing needs of the environment, and the people in it, to reflect those people who make up the companies.

The International Organization for Standardization (ISO), the International-standards setting body, has created a recommendation in an effort to help address the definition of CSR through what it has established in its ISO-26000 guidelines. It states while that it's NOT possible to be ISO-26000-certified, "The overall goal of the ISO 26000 is to help users/organizations behave in a more socially responsible way and thereby contribute more sustainable environmental, social, economic development." It is also intended to aid in helping companies in the sustainable development. It helps in competitive advantage, reputation, ability to attract and attain workers, employee morale, commitment, and productivity.

It all starts with a plan. Your company needs a plan followed by a strategy on how you will execute this plan. Perhaps a little caution. You will struggle with a little FUD (fear, uncertainty, and doubt). That's common, since chances are you are farther along in the process than you think.

Embracing change is not easy, but it comes down to having the right people, process, technology, vision, and foresight to see a decade ahead. Again, like Covey said, "have an end in mind."

Many struggle with that concept, but understanding the goals, and then creating a strategic approach that allows you to pivot as your business and our environment changes. This means, having a team that sees the purpose for less extraction and more financial performance.

Making the Case

Investing in pilot projects, for instance, is a great way to gain real-world experience and educate yourself in a hands-on, relatively low risk setting, as well as gain consumer feedback along the way. Companies need to prepare themselves for the change that is on the horizon and to educate employees on the new technology. In addition, the investments are not cheap to invest in pilot projects. The faster you engage, the faster you can learn to improve. For most companies, that means taking the cue of failing fast and failing quickly so your company can adjust and not fall behind competitively in the face of all these changes.

Companies need to work to educate and strengthen collaboration between partners externally line-of-business, and IT and OT resources internally. Communication in route to achieving sustainability targets is critical to success.

By creating cross-functional teams and making sustainability part of everyday goals, success is greatly enhanced and will ensure key stakeholders are brought together when using new technology and how to deploy solutions to be effective in the field.

It's critical companies use data to their advantage. Monitoring and analytics will transform processes and reveal inefficient areas or opportunities companies should evaluate in greater detail. The smart companies are mastering technology to create new solutions that leverage expansive infrastructure of our existing product design for the ecosystem.

It is more than a convergence of our existing environment, IoT and data, it is a merging of young and old, creating the next exciting synergies through a new lens that we could only imagine. It's all about tapping into technology with the innovation to find new and better ways to make them more productive, efficient, and competitive.

So, let's recap. Since 2007, more than half the world's population has been living in cities, and the United Nations is still projecting 60% by the end of the decade. Cities and metropolitan areas contribute to 60% of the global GDP, and they also account for about 70% of global carbon emissions and some 60% of resource use.

By 2050, that number is expected to spike to almost 70% — nearly seven out of every 10 people worldwide will be living in an urban environment. The need to address these emissions, food security, urbanization; sustainability is no longer an option, but an imperative. Don't forget we already discussed the world population will climb from 7.7 billion people today to a 9.7 billion by 2050, so says the U.N.

At this point, we have taken a deep dive into many topics. If there is one thing as a society we need to work together to comprehend the bigger picture, recognizing there is no one answer to reduce our carbon footprint. The transformation that would be required to limit 1.5 °C means us all considering major tradeoffs between mitigation, adaption, sustainability, and circularity.

There are significant trade-offs in geophysical, environmental, technical, social, economic, cultural, governmental, and institutional that are now required through the unifying lens of the Anthropocene. It's still very difficult for many to understand the profound impact they have on the ecosystem. This global interconnectivity of the past, present, and future of human relations is what is necessary to achieve the Paris Agreement and other sustainability objectives.

Nature needs to be at the center because future generations are at stake. Let's focus on a green recovery because we can have the ability for more sustainable land use. If China can declare to honor the Paris Agreement for a greener commitment, then there is no better time than the present to strive for more circularity. If we all work for Mother Earth, we create more recipes to encourage food security and sustainability.

If there is one thing I have learned from all of this research, if we are talking about natural resources, people, and everything in between, we cannot affect change, but we can restore harmony. Simply, our natural ecosystem will **always be changing**. Just like we are evolving as species— humankind—so will the climate. But we can do better in how we are treating the planet to which we occupy for each generation. But we must work together, generation with generation. We each have something to contribute, only if we are all willing to listen.

References

Acre. (2020) *How Can Successful Stewardship Be Meaningfully Reported?* Accessed
13/July/2020, https://www.acre.com/thought- leadership/how-can-successful-
stewardship-be-meaningfully-reported

Adriaens, Peter. Interview. By Peggy Smedley July 2020

Alden Robinson, Phil (Director). (1989). FIELD OF DREAMS [Film].

Amazon, accessed 12 August 2020, The Climate Pledge (aboutamazon.com)

Bechtel, accessed 26 August 2020, https://www.bechtel.com/

Biography, accessed 07 July 2020, https://www.biography.com/scholar/john-dewey

Black & Veatch, accessed 05 July 2020, https://www.bv.com/

Boulding, Kenneth E. (1966). *The Economics of the Coming   Spaceship Earth.*
http://www.ub.edu/prometheus21/articulos/obspro
metheus/BOULDING.pdf

Bruder, Daniel M. (2020). *The Blendification System.* Routledge.

Circle Economy. (2019). *The Circularity Gap Report.* https://www.circle-
economy.com/resources/the-circularity-gap-report-2019

Circle Economy. (2020). *Creating City Portraits.* https://www.circle-
economy.com/resources/creating-city-portraits

CHA. (2019). 2019 Sustainability Report.
chacompanies.com/default/assets/File/CHA%20Susta
inability%20Plan_Interactive_FINAL.pdf

Climate Change AI. (2019). *Tackling Climate Change with Machine Learning.*
https://www.climatechange.ai/paper#page=7&zoom =auto,0,725

Covey, Stephen R. (2004). *The 7 Habits of Highly Effective People.* Free Press.

Davis, Kimberly. (2018). *Brave Leadership.* Greenleaf Book Group Press.

DiJulius III, John R. (2019). *The Relationship Economy, Building Stronger Customer Connected in
the Digital Age.* Greenleaf
Book Group Press.

Dominican Sisters of Adrian, Michigan, accessed 14, August 2020
http://adriandominicans.org/

Edison International. (2017). *The Clean Power and Electrification Pathway.*
https://www.edison.com/home/our-perspective/clean-power-and-electrification-
pathway.html

Ellen MacArthur Foundation, accessed June 2020
https://www.ellenmacarthurfoundation.org/
Ellen MacArthur Foundation. *Cities and Circular Economy for Food.* Accessed 08,
June 2020 https://www.ellenmacarthurfoundation.org/assets/d
ownloads/Cities-and-Circular-Economy-for-Food_280119.pdf

EPA. *Landfill Methane Outreach Program (LMOP).*
https://www.epa.gov./lmop/basic-information-about-landfill-gas#methane

EPA. *National Oil and Hazardous Substances Pollution Contingency Plan (NCP) Overview.*
https://www.epa.gov/emergency-   response/national-oil-and-hazardous-
substances-pollution-contingency-plan-ncp-overview

EPA. *Summary of the Clean Water Act.* https://www.epa.gov/laws-
regulations/summary-clean-water-act

European Commission, accessed 21 August 2020, https://ec.europa.eu/info/index_en

Food and Agriculture Organization of the United Nations, accessed March 2020
http://www.fao.org/home/en/

Frank and Oak, accessed November 2020, https://www.frankandoak.com/

George, Sam. Interview. By Peggy Smedley. March 2020.

Gerstein, Daniel M. (2019). *The Story of Technology: How We Got Here and What the Future Holds.* Prometheus.

Gartner (2020, October 8). *Gartner Identifies Three Trends That Will Impact the Future of Supply Chain* [Press release]. https://www.gartner.com/en/newsroom/press-releases/2020-10- 08-gartner-identifies-three-trends-that-will-impact-the-future-of-supply-chain

GCP Applied Technologies, interview August 2020. https://gcpat.com/en

Genesis 1: 28-30

Global System for Mobile Communications Association (GSMA), accessed October 2020, https://www.gsma.com/

Guggenheim, Davis (Director). (2006). *An Inconvenient Truth* [Film].

Hungry Harvest, accessed August 2020 https://www.hungryharvest.net/

IBM Food Trust, accessed October 2020 https://www.ibm.com/blockchain/solutions/food-trust

ISO, accessed 10, October 2020, https://www.iso.org/

Jaffe, Dennis R. (2020). *Borrowed from Your Grandchildren: The Evolution of 100-Year Family Enterprises.* Wiley.

Kunzig, Robert. (2020). Is a world without trash possible? *National Geographic.* https://www.nationalgeographic.com/magazine/2020 /03/how-a-circular-economy-could-save-the-world-feature/

LafargeHolcim, accessed October 2020, https://www.lafargeholcim.com/

Library of Congress. *Oil and Gas Industry: A Research Guide, Oil Spills and Gas Leaks.* https://guides.loc.gov/oil-and-gas- industry/controversies/oil-spills

Library of Congress. *Oil and Gas Industry: A Research Guide, Upstream: Production and Exploration.* https://guides.loc.gov/oil-and-gas-industry/upstream

Lux Research. (2020). *Making Sense of "Sustainability."* https://www.luxresearchinc.com/hubfs/2020%20Sustainability%20Campaign/Lux%20Research%20-%20Making%20Sense%20of%20Sustainability%20Whit epaper.pdf

Mars Corporation, accessed 19 July 2020, https://www.mars.com/

Matthew 4:18

McDonough, William & Braungart, Michael. (2002). *Cradle to Cradle* REMAKING THE WAY WE MAKE THINGS. NORTH POINT PRESS.

McKay, Brett & Kate. (2020). How the Generational Cycle of History Explains Our Current Crisis. *The Art of Manliness.* https://www.artofmanliness.com/articles/strauss-howe-Sgenerational-cycle-theory/

Merriam-Webster, accessed 10 August 2020 https://www.merriam-webster.com/

Microsoft, accessed November 2020, https://www.microsoft.com/en-us/

Miller-Brown, Monica. Interview. By Peggy Smedley. June 2020.

Misfits Markets, accessed 20 July 2020, https://www.misfitsmarket.com/

References

NASA (2020, January 15). *NASA, NOAA Analyses Reveal 2019 Second Warmest Year on Record* [Press release]. https://www.nasa.gov/press-release/nasa-noaa-analyses-reveal-2019-second-warmest-year-on-record

Nelson Institute Center for Climatic Research at the University of Wisconsin–Madison, accessed 9 October 2020, https://nelson.wisc.edu/ccr/

NEOM, accessed 11 November 2020, https://www.neom.com/en-us/

NextWave plastic consortium, accessed 11, https://www.nextwaveplastics.org/

Nguyen, Tam. Interview. By Peggy Smedley. 26, August 2020.

OLIO, accessed, September 2020 https://olioex.com/

Perna, Mark C. (2008). *Answering Why.* Greenleaf Book Group Press.

Pew Research Center. (2019). *Mobile Fact Sheet.* https://www.pewresearch.org/internet/fact-sheet/mobile/

Permaculture Principles, accessed August 2020.   https://permacultureprinciples.com/

Pisani, Dr. Francis. (2020). United Nations Educational, Scientific and Cultural Organization (UNESCO). *Smart about Cities: Forging Links for the Future.* https://netexplo.com/static/media/uploads/uploads/pdf/francis_pisani_-_smart_about_cities_ang.pdf

Purdue University. *Generational Differences in the Workplace.* https://www.purdueglobal.edu/

Race to Zero, accessed 21 November 2020 https://racetozero.unfccc.int/

Rocky Mountain Institute, accessed September 2020 https://rmi.org/about/

Roff, Peter. (2020). Righty fury at Fox News is just conservative fratricide. *New York Post.*

Roop, Heidi. Interview. By Peggy Smedley. September 2020

Sanders, Corinne. Interview. By Peggy Smedley. August 2020.

Senate Democrats' Special Committee on the Climate Crisis. (2020). *The Case for Climate Action: Building a Clean Economy for the American People.* https://www.schatz.senate.gov/imo/media/doc/SCCC_Climate_Crisis_Report.pdf

ShareWaste, accessed 27, October 2020, https://sharewaste.com/

Signify, accessed 17 March 2020, https://www.signify.com/en-us

Smart Electric Power Alliance. (2020). *Utility Roadmap to EV Infrastructure Success.* https://sepapower.org/resource/best-practices-for-utility-ev-infrastructure-deployment/

Smedley, Rose. Interview. By Peggy Smedley. 7 Mar 2020

Spathies, William. Interview. By Peggy Smedley. 16 May 2020

Spector, Robert & McCarthy, Patrick (2012). *The Nordstrom   Way to Customer Service Excellence.* Wiley.

Strauss, William & Howe, Neil. (1997). *The Fourth Turning: An American Prophecy – What the Cycles of History Tell Us About America's Next Rendezvous with Destiny.* Crown.

Tam Nguyen, 26/August/2020, The views, thoughts, and   opinions expressed in the case study belong solely to him and not necessarily his employer.

Target Desso, accessed November 2020, Tarkett Group – a global leader in innovative and sustainable solutions for flooring and sports surfaces | Tarkett

The Drawdown Review. *(2020). Climate Solutions for a New Decade.* A Project Drawdown Publication.

https://drawdown.org/sites/default/files/pdfs/The
DrawdownReview%E2%80%932020%
E2%80%93Download.pdf

The Intergovernmental Panel on Climate Change (IPCC), accessed 30 August 2020,
https://www.ipcc.ch/

The National Academics of Sciences Engineering Medicine. (2007). *Global Environmental Health in the 21st Century: From Governmental Regulation to Corporate Social Responsibility: Workshop Summary.* Chapter: 5 Corporate Social Responsibility.
https://www.nap.edu/read/11833/chapter/8

The Network for Greening the Financial System (NGFS), accessed 24 September 2020
https://www.ngfs.net/en

Monica Miller Brown, Interview. By Peggy Smedley. 16,   June 2020

Thyssenkrupp, Elevator https://www.thyssenkrupp.com/en/home 16, June
2020

U.S. Department of Agriculture (USDA). (2020). *Rural Development.*
https://www.rd.usda.gov/sites/default/files/RD_Rec
reation_Economy_USDA.pdf

U.S. Green Building Council (USGBC), accessed 31, July 2020,
https://www.usgbc.org/

United Nations. *Perspectives on social cohesion – the glue that holds society together.*
https://www.un.org/development/desa/en/news/policy/perspectives-on-social-cohesion.html

United Nations. Department of Economic and Social Affairs Sustainable Development. *The 17 Goals.* https://sdgs.un.org/goals

United Nations Framework Convention on Climate Change (UNFCCC), accessed 21, August,
2020   https://unfccc.int/

University of Michigan, accessed 21 August 2020 https://umich.edu/

University of Minnesota, accessed 21 August 2020 https://twin-cities.umn.edu/

Vimont, Daniel. Interview. By Peggy Smedley. September   2020

Walton, Michael. Interview. By Peggy Smedley. September   2020.

Warp + Weft, accessed 4 November 2020, https://warpweftworld.com/

Welch, Jack. (2001) *Jack Straight from the Gut,* Warner Books (Interview)

World Resources Institute. *Greenhouse Gas Protocol.* https://ghgprotocol.org/

World Resources Institute. (2019). *Estimating and Reporting the Comparative Emissions Impacts of Products.* https://www.wri.org/publication/estimating-and-reporting-comparative-emissions-impacts-products

WRAP Waste and Resources Action Programme, accessed 21 August 2020,
https://wrap.org.uk/

WRAP. (2020). *Considerations for Compostable Plastic Packaging.*
https://www.wrap.org.uk/sites/files/wrap/Considerations-for-compostable-plastic-packaging.pdf

WRI Brasil. (2020). *A New Economy For a New Era: Elements for Building a More Efficient and Resilient Economy in Brazil.* https://wribrasil.org.br/pt/publicacoes/new-   economy-brazil-efficient-resilient-build-back-better

Yale University. (2019). *Yale releases 2019 progress on Yale Sustainability Plan 2025.*
https://sustainability.yale.edu/news/yale-releases-2019-progress-yale-sustainability-plan-2025

ACKNOWLEDGMENTS

Many have guided my thinking through deep conversations and collaborations. Few however have had such an impact as these individuals whose friendship and counsel over the years has helped make this book possible. I want to personally thank Sam George, Jim Kissane, Tim Lindner, Dennis Jaffe, John Smedley, Brooke Banbury, Keith Churchill, Tam Nyugen, and Peter Adraiens.

I also want to thank my editors and production team Laura Black, Lynne Flakus, Dave Smedley, Nate Anderson, and Jennifer Zoellick. It was their critical eyes that put the final period in this book.

A

ability, 4, 6, 12, 34, 36, 39, 51–53, 59–61, 126, 131, 148, 192, 195
accord, 141, 143
address climate change, 125, 139
address sustainability, 69
address water scarcity, 127
admixtures, 85–86
  water-reducing concrete, 85
adoption, 46–48
Advanced Research Projects Agency Network, 50
age
  digital, 1, 183–84
  ice, 133–34
Agreement, Paris, 65, 139–41, 143, 145, 195
air, 82, 91, 124, 131, 142, 171, 173
aisle, 56–57
Amazon, 44, 50–54, 57, 59, 82
Amazon Effect, 49, 102
Amazon leader Jeff Bezos, 57
American history, 19, 24–25, 28–29
American society, 33
Apple iPad, 48–49
applications, 48, 50, 157–58
archetypes, generational, 18
Atlantic Ocean, 72
atmosphere, 62, 66, 132, 138, 146, 172–73

B

Baby Boomer generation, 24
Baby Boomers, 16, 24–25, 36, 163–64, 181
Baby Boomers and Millennials, 25
Bechtel, 100–102, 150, 154–56, 160–62
Bechtel family values, 160
Bechtel project and environmental engineer, 101
Bechtel's project team, 154, 156
Bechtel works, 161
Best Buy, 125
biodiversity, 2, 79, 110, 155, 174, 189
birth, 9, 19–20, 23, 25, 34, 58
brands, 16, 34–35, 43–45, 53, 55–56, 84, 152

brands and retailers, 53, 55
building, 8, 10, 41–42, 45, 68, 71, 100, 102, 105, 138–39, 156–57, 159, 173, 186–87
  zero, 173–74
building materials, 139, 156
businesses, 3, 6, 8, 50, 53, 82, 84, 116–18, 129, 171, 178, 180–82, 185–86, 191, 193
business owners, 84

C

campus, 105–7, 122
carbon, 62–63, 66, 69, 83, 125, 142, 153, 171–74
  embodied, 138
  operational, 138
  reducing, 101
  zero, 122, 172, 174
carbon dioxide, 85, 132, 138, 171
  removing, 172
carbon emissions, 125, 133, 157
  global, 109, 194
  reducing, 85
  zero, 139
carbon footprint, 99, 138–39, 157, 195
carbon goals, 174
carbon load, 138
carbon neutrality, 172
carbon reduction, 13, 41
carbon sequestration, 189
cases, 56, 59, 78, 87, 156, 159, 186, 188, 193
CEES (Center for Energy Efficiency and Sustainability), 152–53
CEES works, 152
cement, 85, 139
cement manufacturing, 85
century, 46–47, 72, 76, 84, 118, 133, 139, 147
challenges, 5–6, 9, 11, 27–28, 38, 93, 136, 149, 182, 191
  environmental, 130
children, 24, 30, 37, 43, 49, 89, 154, 176
China, 18, 20, 63, 136, 140–42, 171, 195

circular economy, 2, 12–13, 16, 39, 42, 45, 60, 62–66, 98–99, 101, 104, 150, 152, 168, 170
circularity, 41, 62, 65–66, 68–70, 84–86, 101, 168, 171, 183, 186–87, 195
cities, 64, 67, 94, 97, 104, 108–10, 168, 173, 181–84, 189, 194
civilizations, 13–14
Clean Water Act (CWA), 78
climate change, 5, 9, 36–37, 39, 62–63, 79, 81–82, 84, 134, 140, 142–48, 150, 168–69
  addressed, 132
  ever-changing, 122
  global, 141
  improving, 138
  pre-industrial, 64
climate change data, 144
climate problem, 15
climate science, 146
climate systems, 145–46
closed-loop plastics, 92–93
clothing, 76, 94–95
clothing companies, 95
CO$_2$, 65, 85, 133–34, 138
CO$_2$ emissions, 63, 126, 139, 156–58
  industrial, 85
  reducing, 64
coal, 73–75, 141–43
coal plants, 141
coal production, 141
coffee cups, 91
communities, 2, 5–7, 9–10, 67–68, 97, 99–101, 107, 109–10, 146–48, 150, 152, 154–56, 159–62, 165–66, 189–90
  sustainable, 156, 190
companies, 7–10, 42–43, 66, 75–78, 99–100, 102–4, 114–19, 123, 128–30, 135–37, 148–50, 152–55, 160, 162–63, 165–66, 171–74, 177–78, 180, 186–88, 192–93
  best, 128, 149
  helping, 129, 192
  opportunities, 194
components, 1–2, 93, 103
computers, 30, 48, 51, 92–93, 124

connections, 32, 156
construction, 100, 139, 141, 149
construction materials, 156
consumers, 45, 49–53, 56–57, 62, 74–76, 88–90, 97, 111, 113, 119, 123, 126
consumption, 61, 102–3, 142, 169, 177
core values, 164–65
corporate sustainability, 16, 116, 128
  strong, 128
corporations, 15–16, 126, 192
countries, 31, 64–65, 76, 81, 97–100, 106, 138–41, 143, 145, 166, 169, 171, 173–74
COVID-19 pandemic, 14, 29, 31, 79–80, 136, 148
cradle, 65, 69, 95–96, 130
creation, 87, 108
crises, 18, 20, 30, 40, 67, 75, 148–50
crops, 86–87, 105, 146
CSR (corporate, social, responsibility), 112–13, 115–16, 128–29, 150, 160, 192
customers, 44, 50, 52, 55–57, 59, 70–71, 116–17, 150–51, 153, 155, 161, 172, 175, 177, 179
CWA (Clean Water Act), 78

D
decisions, 7, 11, 43, 45, 120, 154–55, 160
design, 1–2, 6–7, 61, 63–64, 100, 102, 158, 165, 168, 174–75, 181, 184–87
design products, 187
destruction, environmental, 12, 149, 168–69
development, 7, 14, 100, 105, 109, 129, 143, 153
devices
  connected, 29, 34, 48, 103
  personal computer, 49
  wireless, 58–59
digital natives, 30–31, 34
digital twin, 102, 179, 185
direction, 40, 62–63
disruption generation, 30
distribution centers, 55, 57, 59

Index

diversity, 13–14, 30, 36, 41–42, 127, 149
Dominican Sisters, 105–7
droughts, 4–5, 80, 82, 145

E
earth, 9, 65, 72, 75, 81, 91–92, 105, 107, 132, 142, 178
Earth's climate, 79–80, 132
ecological sustainability patterns, 10
ecosystems, 3, 5, 13, 20, 146–47, 163, 170, 175–76, 178, 190, 194–95
ecosystem services, 155
electricity, 74, 117, 122, 158
elevator companies, 71
elevators, 64–65, 68–71
emissions, 70, 116–17, 132–33, 138–39, 141, 153, 171, 174, 184, 195
  methane, 66, 90
employees, 1, 8, 11, 82, 116, 128–29, 149–50, 152, 160, 162–63, 165
endowments, 120–22
energy, 6, 10–11, 13, 68, 95, 100, 138, 153, 156, 173–74, 184
  zero, 173
energy companies, 120
energy consumption, 69, 157
energy regeneration, 68
environment, 2–3, 6, 8, 37–39, 41, 60–61, 63, 92–95, 113–14, 131–33, 154–56, 160, 175–76, 186, 192
environmental benefits, 86, 138, 170
environmental impact, 116, 128, 155, 163
environmentalists, 3, 12, 82, 141–42
ESG (environmental, social, governance), 1, 8, 69, 112, 114–15, 123, 153, 191
European-based companies, 115

F
factories, 62, 72, 74–75, 77, 82, 176, 178, 186
family, 23–24, 27, 89, 116, 149, 151
FAO (Food and Agriculture), 66–67, 88, 90, 109
farm, 86, 88, 105–6, 176, 186
farmers, 22, 87, 89

Fenner, 169
First World War, 73
food, 3, 13, 53–54, 66–67, 76, 86–92, 97, 103, 105–6, 108–9, 111
  grown, 106
Food and Agriculture Organization, 88, 109
food choices, 104
food loss, 88–90
food manufacturers, 104
food manufacturers conduct, 182
food production, 67, 109, 145
food products, 104
food scraps, 91
food security, 107, 195
food waste, 66–67, 86, 88–90, 96, 101, 104
Ford, Henry, 73
fork, 168, 176, 181
fossil fuels, 103, 121, 124, 140, 142–43
Fourth Turning, 17–18, 20, 45
France, 47, 98–99
fruits, 87–88, 106, 108

G
Generational Differences, 20
generational eras, 20
generation experiences, 19
generations, 14–31, 35–41, 43, 45, 47, 80, 83, 110–12, 125, 127–28, 130, 168, 170, 191–92, 195–96
  engaged, 17, 54
  first, 17, 29–30
  five, 15–16, 21, 40
  largest, 24, 26
  new, 19, 151
  next, 11, 14, 42, 67, 79, 113, 164, 168
generative families, 2, 128, 148, 150–51, 165
globe, 13, 17, 31, 36, 48, 75–77, 82, 173, 176
goals, 38, 41, 63–65, 98–99, 107, 152–53, 160, 171–72, 182–83, 187, 192–93
goods, 56, 73–76, 96–97, 117, 161, 178
governance, 8, 112, 114, 152–53

governments, 3, 6–7, 9, 11, 15, 62–63, 78, 81, 134–35, 167–68, 171, 174, 181
Greatest Generation, 21–23, 28
group, 24–26, 31, 40

H
history, 7, 15, 18–22, 24, 26, 36, 46–59, 73, 110–11, 152, 175
homes, 22–23, 29–30, 35, 52, 90, 97, 117, 124, 159, 170, 176
Howe, 18–19, 25, 27, 29, 45
HP, 93, 123, 125
Hungry Harvest, 87–88

I
IBM Food Trust, 89
Ice Age Problem, 134
India, 141–42
individuality, 40–41
individuals, 2–3, 5–6, 9, 20, 24, 26, 62, 64, 90–91, 116, 130–31, 167–68, 171
Industrial Revolution, 13, 20, 47, 62, 72, 75, 169–70
industries, 7, 9, 11, 71, 74–76, 157, 164, 168, 174, 182, 185
  new, 60
infrastructure, 22, 47, 139, 148, 184–85
innovation, 1–2, 7–8, 27, 47, 56, 86–87, 152, 186, 188–89, 194
Intergovernmental Panel on Climate Change. *See* IPCC
internet, 20, 29–30, 49–51, 102, 183
investment, 115, 122, 127, 135, 150, 152–54, 156, 193
IoT (Internet of Things), 102, 179, 182–85, 187, 194
IPCC (Intergovernmental Panel on Climate Change), 64, 81
iPhone, first-generation, 48
Iran, 141–42
Iraq, 28, 141–42
irrigate, 4
ISO, 192
ISVs, 162–63
items, 84, 89, 178–79, 182

J
jeans, 94, 166

L
LafargeHolcim, 157–58
land, 4, 75, 78, 91, 105–6, 108, 142, 171, 174, 189–90
landfills, 3, 62–63, 82, 86, 90, 93–95, 101, 132, 142, 153, 179
leaders
  next-generation, 60
  sustainability programs, 153
Leadership in Energy and Environmental Design (LEED), 159
learning, 42, 107, 137–38, 175
LEED (Leadership in Energy and Environmental Design), 159
leveraging sustainability efforts, 158
life, quality of, 2, 159, 191–92
local communities, 7, 129, 160–61
location, 52, 56–57, 59, 100
long-term sustainability, 118
low-carbon agenda, 65

M
machines, 47, 51, 73, 117, 170
make-take-waste world, 168
manufacture, products companies, 122
manufacturers, 43–44, 62, 76, 102–3, 131, 136–37, 164–65, 185
manufacturing, 18, 43, 47, 73, 82, 138, 149, 163–65, 185
market, 48–49, 54, 57
marketing, digital, 44
Mars, 118–19
mCommerce, 50–53, 57
media, social, 29, 31, 35–36, 44–45, 48
Michigan, 105–6, 119–20, 122
Microsoft, 43, 162–63, 172, 179
Midwest, 146–47
military, 18, 23, 28
Millennial generation, 26
Millennials, 16–17, 25–26, 28, 33–34, 36–38, 43–45, 163–65, 191
Miller Brown, 64, 69–71

Index

Mining Sustainability, 159
Misfits Markets, 87–88
models, economic, 144
monetary policy, 144
monitors, 92–93, 103, 143, 184
monitor sustainability processes, 10
movement, 96, 120, 123, 166, 168
multigenerational, 39
multi-generations, 36
music, 26, 31

N
NASA, 132–33
National Contingency Plan (NCP),
    78
National Oceanic and Atmospheric
    Administration (NOAA), 132–
    33
natural environment, 11, 109–10, 165,
    168, 181
natural resources, 2–3, 6, 8–9, 62–63,
    72, 75, 86, 95, 102–3, 131, 135
NCP (National Contingency Plan),
    78
NEOM, 189–90
net, 83, 122, 139, 171, 173–74, 183
New Deal in World War II, 19
NGFS, 143–44
Nguyen, 100–101, 162
NOAA (National Oceanic and
    Atmospheric Administration),
    132–33

O
oceans, 3–4, 6, 62, 82, 122–25, 142,
    146, 152, 181
OLIO app, 90
OneCem, 157–58
on-site, 173–74
OPEC (Organization of Petroleum
    Exporting Countries), 142
operations, 77, 121, 137, 152–53, 158,
    162, 186
order fulfillment, 52, 57
order selection, 58
Organization of Petroleum
    Exporting Countries (OPEC),
    142

organizations, 8–9, 11, 13, 116, 123,
    125, 128–29, 136, 138, 142–43,
    152, 182, 187

P
packaging, 89, 123, 125
packaging sustainability, 182
pandemic, 11, 20, 29–30, 49, 54, 68,
    80, 87, 94, 136, 148–49
parents, 18, 26, 29–30, 37, 43
passion, 39, 42, 44, 61, 149
performance, financial, 115, 193
performance standards, 58
permaculture, 105–8, 110
pillars, 7, 114, 125, 127
planet, 4, 9, 75, 79, 93–95, 97, 117–19,
    128, 130, 132, 139
plants, 72, 85, 91, 103–4, 155, 158, 164
plastics, 3, 62, 82, 93, 97, 119, 122,
    124, 142, 152
    recycled, 125
plastics consortium, 123–24
pollution, 2, 4, 62, 65–66, 72, 77, 140,
    142, 190
population, world's, 5, 86, 102, 109,
    194
Portland cement, 156–57
pre-industrial levels, 139–40
President Trump, 140–41, 143
principles, 2, 62, 66, 98, 108–9, 124,
    128
product design, 2, 194
production
    mass, 73–74
    world's copper, 161
product-oriented approach, 97, 177
products, 2–3, 52–53, 55–57, 59, 62,
    71, 73–75, 85–86, 89, 93, 96–97,
    102, 119, 123–25, 129–30, 151–
    52, 157, 177–78
    petroleum-based, 142
    plastic, 142
    returned customer, 179
    right, 70–71
products customers, 175
profits, 118, 127–28, 130
projects, 2, 40, 100–101, 120, 151, 154–
    55, 160–62, 182, 189

purchase, 48, 51–53, 55, 57, 94, 111,
    117, 173, 178

R
rainfall events, 146–47
Red Sea, 189
regions, 4, 92, 146
renewable energy, 122, 158, 172–74,
    190
rent, 97, 170, 176
repurposing, 92–93, 97, 176
reputation, 15, 129, 154, 192
research, 55, 131–33, 153, 196
resources, 2, 5–6, 27, 72, 107–9, 112,
    152–53, 178
responsibility, corporate social, 113,
    115–16, 128, 150, 191
restaurants, 104
result, 26, 33, 35, 77–79, 81, 87, 89, 93,
    109, 121, 123, 128, 131
retailers, 43–44, 52–53, 55, 57, 104
reuse, 63, 65, 69, 95–96
reusing, 92
risks, 8, 81, 147–48
roadmap, 98–99, 108, 159

S
Saudi Arabia, 142, 189
Saudi economy, 189
science, 23, 78, 169–70
SCMs, 157
scope, 47, 49, 114, 116–17
Screeners, 30, 33, 36
SDGs (sustainable development
    goals), 113, 187
selectors, human, 58–59
sensors, 103, 184
services, 15, 52, 75, 93–97, 99, 109,
    129, 143, 161, 175–78
set sustainability goals, 125
Shanghai World Financial Center, 69
shift, generational, 130
shop, 52–53, 152
showrooming, 52, 55
Silent Generation, 16, 23
Simon, 51, 83
sisters, 105–7
smartphones, 34, 46, 48, 51, 53, 55

social sustainability, 101
soils, 61, 86, 103–4, 107, 174
solar array, 158
solutions, 69–71, 102, 107, 143, 150,
    179
states, 52, 97–98, 106, 143, 146, 192
Stewardship Across Generations, 127
success, 7, 14, 42, 56, 98, 107, 118,
    182–83, 193–94
supply chains, 42–43, 50, 57, 87, 94,
    117, 123, 129, 135–37, 152, 165
sustainability, 1, 7, 11–13, 44–45, 62–
    168, 171, 174, 180, 182–83, 187,
    189, 191, 195
    environmental, 167
    maintaining, 137
sustainability action plan, 42, 153
sustainability commitments, 152, 171
sustainability conversation, 112, 127
sustainability efforts, 8
    bold, 152
sustainability goals, 152, 164, 182–83,
    187
sustainability impacts, real, 165
sustainability initiatives, 137
sustainability innovation, 69
sustainability issues, 115
sustainability methods, better, 67
sustainability mission, 11, 190
sustainability objectives, 153, 174,
    195
sustainability paradigm, 127
sustainability plans, strong, 128
sustainability principles, 10
sustainability problems, 6
sustainability programs, 190
sustainability report, 44
sustainability strategy, 182
Sustainability Tam Nguyen, 100, 161
sustainability targets, 193
sustainable development goals
    (SDGs), 113, 187
sustainable ecosystem, 2
sustainable world, 33, 60
systems, 58, 62, 66, 108–10, 146, 181,
    185
    developing comprehensive
        sustainability management, 162

Index

T

tablets, 30, 35, 48, 51
technology, 2, 5, 26–27, 30, 32, 47, 49, 76, 78, 179, 181, 184, 193–94
innovative, 12, 126
new, 10, 58, 193–94
thinking, 64, 66, 102, 107, 130, 135, 140–41, 163, 170, 187
generational, 128
Thyssenkrupp Elevator, 64, 68–71
tons, 82, 85–86, 157–58
Traditionalists, 16–17, 23–24, 27, 36
Trane Technologies, 152–53
transformation, digital, 125–26, 179, 181, 183
transitioning, 121–22, 162
transportation, 9, 13, 82, 89, 138–39, 161, 184
trucks, 56–57, 85–87
Turning, 12, 17, 20
types, 26, 54, 60, 66, 80, 103–4, 120, 127

U

underpinnings, 107–8
understanding, 18, 33, 40–42, 82–83, 99, 101, 115, 118–19, 128, 134, 191, 193
UNFCCC (United Nations Framework Convention on Climate Change), 145
United States, 14, 23, 25, 51, 63, 72–73, 80, 90, 99, 140–43, 146
university, 67, 98, 120–22
University of Michigan, 119–20, 122
USGBC (U.S. Green Building Council), 158

V

vegetables, 87–88, 105–6, 108
vision, 33–34, 61, 83, 150, 153, 189, 191, 193

W

Walton, 163–65

waste, 2, 62, 66–67, 74–75, 84, 86, 90–91, 96, 100–101, 104, 174, 177–79, 186
water, 4–6, 10, 72, 75, 77–78, 101, 108–9, 142, 147, 184, 190
water environments, 110
water scarcity, 2, 4–5, 13
water shortages, 5, 9, 39, 75
waterways, 3, 124, 155
Webvan, 53–54
Wisconsin, 146–47
women, 22–23
word sustainability, 112, 116
work, 15, 24–27, 30–31, 40–44, 67–68, 71–72, 80, 99–100, 137, 149–51, 161–62, 169–70, 180, 192–93, 195–96
workforce, 15, 20–21, 30, 41
world, 3–5, 7–8, 12–17, 19–21, 27–29, 35, 37–38, 41–42, 48–49, 63–65, 73–75, 102–3, 141–42, 145–46, 151–52, 160–61, 168–69, 174–76, 179, 181
world leaders, 137, 141
world population, 169, 195
world power, 18–19, 76
World Trade Center Twin Towers, 28
World War I, 73
World War II, 19, 21–22, 24, 77
World Wide, 50
World Wide Waiter, 54

Y

younger generation, 17, 27, 31–32, 34, 37–43, 60, 94, 163, 165, 187, 190–91

Made in the USA
Middletown, DE
15 May 2021

39806982R00126